LEARN ENGLISH THROUGH

Football

LEARN ENGLISH THROUGH
Football

EOGHAN MCGINTY

EAST PIER **PRESS**

www.eastpierpress.com

First published 2017

Author Acknowledgements

I would like to thank my friends and family for their help and support. Special thanks to John McGinty and Ronan Grace for editing the manuscript, and to all the artists for giving me permission to use their works. Special thanks also to Maura McGinty for her unstinting encouragement.

Illustrations by

Dave Merrell (*www.davemerrell.com*): *Zidane, Messi #10, Brian Clough, Maradona, Pele #10, Socrates (back cover)*
Sasha Vetlina (*sashavetlina@gmail.com*): *Cruyff with Pigs*
Charis Tsevis (*www.flickr.com/tsevis*): *C Ronaldo, Messi mosaic ('Messi Fact File', 'Phrasal Verbs'), Adebayor, Eto'o, Del Piero, Pato, Kaka, Ronaldinho mosaic, Falcao)*
Ana Balderramas *(www.behance.net/anabalderramas): Balotelli*
Mathew Vieira (*www.mathewvieira.com*): *Iniesta, Lewandowski, Pogba, Ozil, Neymar, Bale*
Laurence Ventress: *Suarez*
Davide Manna (*www.behance.net/manna87*): *Hamsik*
Luke D'Agostino (*www.behance.net/Luke_Dagostina*): *1994 World Cup final (front cover), Cruyff Legend*
Pete Richardson (*www.peterichardsondesign.com*): *Pele Silhouette*
David Garces(*www.behance.net/davidgarces): Ronaldinho caricature*

Drop us a line at *emgmusic@dublin.com* to request a bonus unit!

Learn English through Football II is coming soon.

Contents

Present Simple and Continuous

> ''Why put another layer of gold paint on the Bentley,' asked Zinedine Zidane when Real Madrid decided to buy Beckham and sell Claude Makelele, 'when **you are losing** the entire engine?''

The **Present Simple** has a few different uses.

We use it:

1 To talk about facts or generally held truths.

*Football matches **last** ninety minutes.*

*Crystal Palace **play** several London derbies every season.*

2 To talk about regular habits or repeated actions.

*Why does Laurent Blanc always **kiss** Fabien Barthez's head before a game starts?*

*Our supporters **get** restless if the team doesn't score an early goal.*

3 To talk about momentary actions.

*Hulk **passes** to Neymar, Neymar **shoots** … and **scores**!*

4 To talk about the future.

   a after conjunctions

*I'll text you when I **arrive** at the Shankly Gates.*
*I'll always love Maradona, whatever he **does**.*

   b when we talk about schedules and timetables.

*The game **kicks off** at 3 o'clock.*
*The new season **starts** tomorrow.*

5 To give instructions and directions.

*You **log on** to their site, and then you **use** your credit card o buy a ticket.*

6   To talk about a book, film or play or to tell a story or a joke.

   *He **meets** his idol, the club **signs** him, he **scores** the winning goal in the cup final. It's a bit too unrealistic for me. You might like it though.*

To form the **Present Continuous,** we use the present simple form of *to be* along with the main verb in the -ing form**.**

We use it:

1   To talk about actions happening at the moment of speaking.

   *Lacazette **is taking** his time to leave the pitch. He's definitely **time-wasting**.*

2   To talk about things happening 'around now' or temporary situations.

   *Football **is receiving** a lot of negative publicity at the moment.*

   *They**'re playing** their home matches at Wembley while their stadium is being renovated.*

3   To talk about future plans and arrangements.

   *Jason **is holding** a Japanese-themed World Cup party at the weekend. We're all invited.*

4   To talk about changing situations or trends.

   *The price of Champions League tickets **is rising** all the time.*

   *It's **getting** harder and harder to retain the Champions League. The last team to win the trophy two years in a row was AC Milan, when it was still known as the European Cup.*

5   We can use *always* with the present continuous to mean very often or continually.

   *He's **always kissing** the badge on his jersey and **saying** how much he loves the club, but I wouldn't be surprised if he left us for a bigger club at the end of the season.*

We can use verbs that describe the way we feel physically – ache, feel, hurt – in a simple or continuous form with no change of meaning.

   *My back **hurts**. OR My back **is hurting**.*

   *I **feel** sick. OR I'm **feeling** sick.*

EXERCISE

Insert a word from the box in the right sentence and in the correct form

| mean | lift | use | live | leave | know | be | know | miss | be | watch |

1 After a Maradona-inspired Napoli won the Italian championship in 1987, someone wrote on the city's graveyard wall: 'You don't _____ what you're _____.

2 Jean-Marc Bosman, the former player who the Bosman Ruling is named after, _____ in a small flat in Liège, a recovering alcoholic surviving on £625 a month.

3 Fans across the world _____ the English term *derby* (generally pronounced *der*-by rather than how anglophones pronounce it, *dar*-by) for a local rivalry.

4 'Do you _____ which famous derby is known as the Flu-Fla?''Of course, it's Fluminense v Flamengo, the big Rio derby.'

5 La Masia _____ 'farmhouse' in Catalan.

6 '_____ there really a club in Bolivia called The Strongest?''Yes, and there's a football club in Peru called Lawn Tennis.'

7 'When Germany scored to make it 2-2 in the final, I said to myself, "The Cup is _____ me, no, please, no.' – Maradona, after the Mexico '86 final.

8 Mario Goetze _____ the first substitute in the history of the World Cup to score the winning goal in the final.

9 Cristiano Ronaldo _____ around 23,000 kgs of weight during a typical training session, which is the equivalent of sixteen Toyota Prius cars.

10 'I don't _____ penalties in my hotel room. I watch naughty videos.' – Gianluigi Buffon

Lionel Messi Fact File

Lionel Messi is widely considered the best player of his generation, if not of all time. Here are some interesting facts about him:

Messi's son, Thiago, was born 869 days after the birth of Cristiano Ronaldo Junior. This is the exact same age difference that exists between their fathers (Ronaldo is 869 days older than Messi).

At the age of 11, he was diagnosed with a rare growth hormone deficiency. His parents could no longer afford to pay for his medical treatment. The Sporting Director of FC Barcelona, Carles Rexach, offered to pay the medical bills if Messi moved to Spain and joined Barça.

His 2005 international debut against Hungary lasted just 47 seconds, when he received a red card after coming on as a substitute. He cried all night long.

Messi ranked second behind Neymar in SportsPro magazine's 2013 list of the world's most marketable athletes.

He has been a very shy person right from his childhood.

Japanese jeweller Ginza Tanaka used a cast of Messi's left foot to create a solid gold replica, weighing 25 kgs. It's worth £3.4 million.

He donated €600,000 for the renovation of a children's hospital in Rosario, his hometown.

His nickname is the Flea.

He is 5 feet 7 inches tall.

At three years old, he used to beat all his friends at marbles.

The first time he joined in with his father and brothers in a game of street football, they were completely amazed by how good he was.

In April 2001, as a result of being tackled hard, his left leg was fractured. A week after he had recovered from the broken leg, he tore ankle ligaments while walking down the stairs.

One of his most famous goals is the goal he scored for Barcelona against Getafe in the Copa del Rey. It has been compared to Maradona's second goal against England at the 1986 World Cup.

His favourite Argentinian club is Newell's Old Boys, on whose youth teams he played.

In 2009, he was voted FIFA World Player of the Year and he also won the Ballon d'Or. When these two awards were merged into one to form the FIFA Ballon d'Or, he won this prize in 2010, 2011, 2012 and 2015.

He has won eight La Liga titles with Barcelona, and four Champions Leagues.

He won an Olympic gold medal in 2008.

He has won four Spanish Cups and three FIFA Club World Cups with Barcelona.

He is FC Barcelona's all-time leading goalscorer.

He played his first World Cup match for Argentina against the Netherlands in Frankfurt on 21 June 2006. He had the phrase 'Hand of God 22 June 1986' stitched into his boots, a tribute to Maradona and the infamous goal he scored aginst England almost exactly twenty years earlier.

In 2007, he set up the Leo Messi Foundation with the aim of providing opportunities for disadvantaged youths.

Though it has been said by some observers that he hasn't performed as well for Argentina as he has for Barcelona, he won the FIFA Golden Ball as the best player of the 2014 World Cup.

EXERCISE

Say whether the following sentences are _true_ or _false_ according to the text

1 He's nicknamed after an insect.

2 No Barcelona player has scored more goals for the club than him.

3 He was top scorer at the 2014 World Cup.

4 He's a big Boca Juniors fan.

5 Germany 2006 was his first World Cup.

6 His debut for Argentina lasted less than a minute.

7 He has broken one of his legs before.

8 He didn't mind being sent off on his international debut.

DISCUSSION

Do you think Lionel Messi is the best player of all time?

Is it possible to compare players from different eras?

Present Perfect Simple and Continuous

> **"** All right. Forget what **has** just **happened**. You've **been** the better team. You've **won** the World Cup once. Now go and win it again. **"**

—ENGLAND MANAGER ALF RAMSEY TO HIS PLAYERS BEFORE THE EXTRA TIME PERIOD IN THE 1966 WORLD CUP FINAL. GERMANY HAD SCORED A VERY LATE EQUALISER

The present perfect always shows a connection between the past and now. We do not use it if we are not thinking about the present.

Present Perfect Simple

Positive	Negative	Question
I/you/we/they have played	I/you/we/they haven't played	I/you/we/they played?
he/she/it has played	he/she/it hasn't played	Has he/she/it played?

We use the present perfect simple to talk about a present situation which started in the past.

*He's **been** a United player for six seasons now.*

For is used with periods of time (for: two weeks, ten hours, a hundred years); *since* is used to identify the point at which a period of time began (since: 2 o'clock, Thursday, 1987).

*He **hasn't started** a game since October.*

We also use the present perfect simple for finished actions which have consequences in the present.

*The referee **has sent** him off. Can you believe it?*
(The present consequence is he is no longer on the pitch)

We often use it to talk or ask about life experiences, using *have you ever?*

*'**Have you ever been** to the Nou Camp?'*
'Only for a tour of the stadium, never for an actual match, sadly.'

Before, yet and already are often used in this context too.

It is also used to say that something has happened several times up to the present.

*Ronaldo **has scored** fifty one goals since the start of the season. He's a goal machine, isn't he?*

We use it too to talk about actions and states which started in the past and still continue. (We can also use the present perfect continuous in this way – see below)

*I**'ve followed** Saint-Étienne since I was a kid. The side they had in the 70s was great.*

We often start a point or story in the present perfect, but then switch to the past simple when elaborating. It's not normal to continue using the present perfect. (See below, the quotation in exercise question 9)

Present Perfect Continuous

Positive	Negative	Question
I/you/we/they have been playing	I/you etc haven't been playing	Have I/you been playing?
he/she/it has been playing	he/she/it hasn't been playing	Has he/she been playing?

We prefer the present perfect continuous for more temporary actions and situations which started in the past and which still continue; when we talk about more permanent (long-lasting) situations, we prefer the present perfect simple.

*He **hasn't been playing** very well recently.*

*He **hasn't played well** for years.*

The present perfect continuous emphasises the length of an activity; the present perfect simple focuses on the number of times the activity has occurred.

*He'**s been training** with the reserves for the last six weeks.*

*He'**s played** three times for the reserves.*

The present perfect continuous focuses on the activity itself; it doesn't show if the activity is completed or not. The simple form focuses on the result or the completion of the activity.

*Neymar's representatives **have been negotiating** a new contract for months now.*

*He'**s signed** a new contract.*

Some verbs are not normally used in continuous forms, namely verbs that refer to mental activities (*remember, understand, realise, etc.*) and verbs of the senses (*sound, hear, taste, etc.*)

> If I **'ve understood** correctly the reports which have recently been coming out of the club, it seems that they're about to fire their manager. NOT ~~If I've been understanding…~~

EXERCISE

Complete the sentences with the verbs in the box in the correct form

triumph score have play put admit describe spend be win pay melt

1 Laurent Blanc, Didier Deschamps, Darko Kovačević and Christian Panucci have all _____ in each of the Premier League, Serie A and La Liga.

2 Man Utd fanatic Ray Adler has _____ more than £150,000 collecting Man Utd memorabilia.

3 Lev Yashin is the only goalkeeper ever to have _____ the Ballon d'Or.

4 Sporting Lisbon have always _____ Eusébio's signing to Benfica as a 'kidnap'. They argued that he belonged to them as he'd passed through their satellite club in Lourenco Marques.

5 'It's a lovely ice cream that has been _____ in the sun for the last 16 months.' –Guillem Balague on Barcelona after they lost heavily to Bayern Munich in the Champions League in 2013.

6 'It still rankles with me that he has never really _____ to what he did. He's never really _____ both hands up – the hands of God – and said, 'Yes, it was the wrong thing to do.' – England defender Terry Butcher about Maradona's first goal against England at Mexico '86.

7 The German national team has _____ in every World Cup penalty shootout they've been involved in.

8 'Under Brazilian law, the maximum sentence is 30 years imprisonment, but I have been _____ for 50.' – Moacyr Barbosa, the Brazilian goalie who has always been blamed for his country's defeat against Uruguay in the 1950 World Cup.

9 After Tottenham beat fellow English club Wolves in the final of the 1972 UEFA Cup, their manager Bill Nicholson told his team: 'I've just _____ in the Wolves dressing room. I told them they were the better team. You lot were lucky. The best team lost tonight.'

10 George Best scored six goals against Northampton in an FA Cup tie in 1970. 'Haven't you _____ enough yet?' their keeper said, as Best jogged his way back to his own half after scoring his sixth.

Lights, Camera, Simulation: Staged Diving with Allan Simonsen

It's all too common nowadays to hear people complaining that professional footballers are forever diving; that they pretend to have been fouled in order to win free kicks and penalties, to get opponents booked or sent off, or just to waste time or slow a game down. But supporters usually turn a blind eye when it's one of their own team's players who's responsible for this diving, or 'simulation'.

This may not have been the case with supporters of the Danish national team, however, who would have had good reason to be annoyed with one of their own players, Allan Simonsen, for his extreme act of simulation during a Danish international fixture.

On 1 May 1977, Denmark were playing Poland in a World Cup qualifier in Copenhagen. When one of the home side's players sent a corner kick into the Polish penalty area, many in the crowd must have been puzzled by the way Simonsen threw himself into the air, the player getting nowhere near the football. This bemusement may have turned to anger when the fans learned the truth behind their player's antics.

Director Tom Hedegaard was filming *Skytten* (The Marksman, in English), a movie about a militant activist who kills people in order to alert Denmark to the dangers of nuclear power. He wanted Simonsen to be one of the marksman's high-profile victims. Because of the difficulties and costs involved in re-enacting a football match for film, Hedegaard persuaded Simonsen to simulate being shot during a real game. The player chose this corner kick situation to fake his own death.

Now, you might ask, what's the big deal? It was just a couple of seconds out of a ninety-minute match, what harm did it do? The inconvenient truth, however, is that had Simonsen stayed on his feet a little longer, he was in a great position to head the ball towards the Polish goal (you can see the incident on YouTube, under Allan Simonsen vs Jens Okking). Denmark mightn't have lost the game 2-1, and so might have qualified for the 1978 World Cup in Argentina.

So why did Allan Simonsen – the 1977 European Footballer of the Year and the only player ever to have scored in each of the UEFA Cup final, the Cup Winners Cup final and the European Cup final

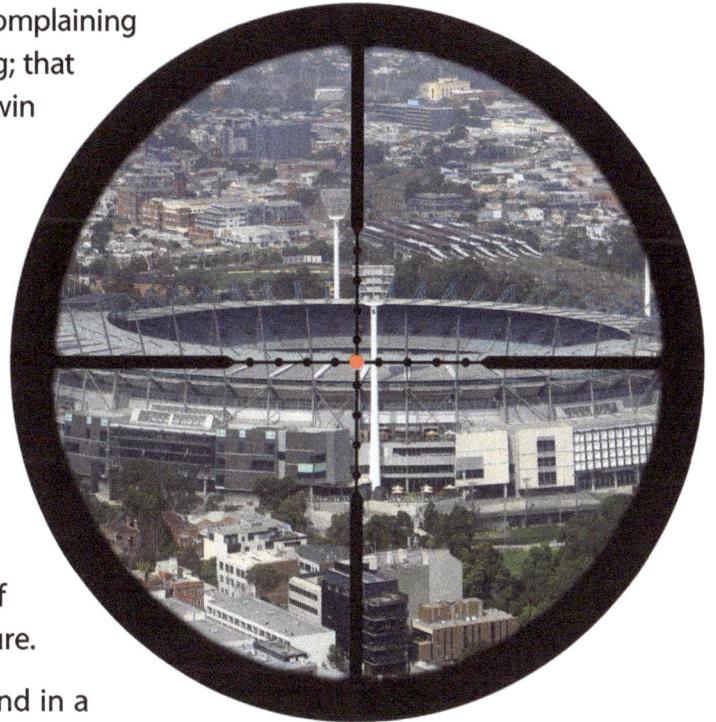

- agree to involve himself in such a project? Was it for the money? Did he support the message of the film? Or was there some other reason? We're not sure.

What we do know is that he hasn't gone on to become another Vinnie Jones or Eric Cantona, two professional footballers who have embarked on long and successful acting careers after hanging up their boots. While he has deservedly been inducted into the Danish Football Association's Hall of Fame, there are no plans afoot to award him his own star on Hollywood Boulevard.

So what became of the movie? Sadly, just like Simonsen in the Polish penalty box, Skytten flopped immediately on launch.

EXERCISE

Find the following in the text:

1   A verb which means to fall clumsily into water or to fail badly. (paragraph 8)

2   A verb which means to pretend to be or do something. (paragraph 4)

3   A noun meaning surprise. (paragraph 3)

4   An expression which means to pretend not to see or be aware of something. (paragraph 1)

5   Another word for damage. (paragraph 5)

6   A verb meaning to bring something to someone's attention. (paragraph 4)

7   A word we use for when a player receives a yellow card from a referee. (paragraph 1)

8   A verb which means to be elected into an institution as recognition for one's achievements. (paragraph 7)

9   An expression which means 'what's the problem?'. (paragraph 5)

10   A noun which means to take-off or to release. (paragraph 8)

> **"** FIFA **cut** my legs **off,** just as I **was proving** to my daughters that I **could** play with 20-year-olds. **"**

–DIEGO MARADONA, AFTER BEING EXPELLED FROM THE USA WORLD CUP, 4 JULY 1994

Past Simple

Positive: verb + -ed (or -d)	Fabio Cannavaro **played** for Napoli.
Negative: did not (didn't) + verb	He **didn't play** for Barcelona.
Question: Did …+ verb?	**Did** he **play** for Juventus?

Note that there are many irregular verbs in English which do not follow the rules in the above box, e.g. the past of *go* is *went* (NOT ~~goed~~), the past of *buy* is *bought* (NOT ~~buyed~~), etc.

We use the past simple

1 when we tell people about past events. We can use it to talk about short, quickly finished actions and events, longer situations and repeated events. Often the time is mentioned.

Ajax ***won*** *the European Cup three years in a row – 1971, 1972 and 1973.*

Ryan Giggs ***retired*** *from professional football in 2014.*

2 to talk about past habits and states. The difference between using the past simple and *used to/would* is that we can state the time with the past simple.

Paolo Maldini ***played*** *for AC Milan for all 25 seasons of his professional career.*

He ***used to play*** *for AC Milan but NOT* ~~*He used to play for AC Milan for 25 seasons*~~*.*

3 to talk about people who are dead.

Bobby Moore ***was*** *the greatest player ever to wear the West Ham jersey.*

4 to give a series of actions in the order that they happened.

Maradona ***took*** *the ball,* ***slalomed*** *past five or six English players,* ***side-stepped*** *Shilton and* ***slid*** *the ball into the back of the net.*

5 in reported speech.

'I'm tired,' he said.

*He said he **was** tired.*

Past Continuous

Positive: was/were + ing-form of the verb

*The supporters **were singing** his name.*

Negative: wasn't/weren't + ing-form of the verb

*They **weren't watching** the match.*

Question: Was/Were … +ing-form of the verb

***Was** he **gesturing** towards them?*

We usually use the past continuous in contrast with the past simple, to describe something which was in progress when the main event(s) of the story happened.

*Antoine Griezmann's sister was in the Bataclan theatre on the night of the November 2015 Paris terrorist attacks, while at the same time Griezmann **was playing** at the Stade de France.*

⚽ DID YOU KNOW? ⚽

When a customer in a Barcelona cafe **mistook** Andrés Iniesta for a waiter, he **went** to the kitchen anyway and **got** her order.

Remember that some verbs are not normally used in continuous forms. Many of these verbs refer to mental activities (e.g. *know, think, believe*) or refer to the senses (e.g. *smell, taste*)

EXERCISE

Change the verbs in the box into the correct tense – past simple or continuous – and then complete the sentences

can	score	choose	be	stand up	remain	claim	ref
meet	insist	thrill	act	carry out	look	perform	find

1 An interesting fact about the 2002 World Cup final was that Brazil and Germany were ____ for the first time in a match in the finals.

2 In a 1999 poll, Barcelona supporters ____ Ladislao Kubala as the greatest Barça player of all time.

3 Considered global football's first superstar, José Andrade once ____ spectators by travelling half the pitch with the ball on his head.

4 A survey ____ ____ by Real Madrid ____ that there are more Real Madrid supporters in Seville than there are for the city's two main clubs, Real Betis and Sevilla, combined.

5 In the early days of radio broadcasting of games in England, the Football League ____ so wary of the effect on attendances that they ____ that the details of which actual match was to be covered ____ secret.

6 When Johann Cruyff signed for Barça in 1973 ahead of Real Madrid he said it was because he ____ never join a club 'associated with Franco'.

7 'I wasn't _____ a football match, I was _____ as an umpire on military manoeuvres,' Ken Aston, the English referee, on officiating the notorious 'Battle of Santiago' World Cup '62 game between Italy and hosts Chile.

8 'The Real Madrid players were _____. They nearly applauded. The stadium was _____ _____. It was the moment Ajax took over. Before then, it was always the big Real Madrid and the little Ajax.' - Gerrie Muhren on his famous ball-juggling cameo during their 1973 European Cup semi-final at the Bernabeu.

9 As a junior player in Norway, Morten Gamst Pedersen _____ six goals directly from corners in the same match.

10 In 2014, Emmanuel Adebayor _____ that his mother was _____ black magic – known as juju – on him, and that was why his goals had dried up.

Rearrange the words in the following sentences to make some of the rules of football

e.g. **Ball**: spherical leather be Must 68-70 cm of made and circumference in.

Answer: Must be spherical, made of leather and 68-70 cm in circumference.

1 **Equipment**: stockings Players a wear shinguards and footwear must jersey shorts.

2 **Method of scoring**: mouth goal ball crosses The the the inside goal line.

3 **Field of play**:

    a played either game natural artificial The can on be or surfaces.

    b rectangular shape green must The in surface be and.

4 **Referee**: are ensures The respected upheld Game the of the and Laws referee.

5 **Throw- in**: touch restart Used whole after play to the of ball the crossed has the line.

6 **Start and restart of play**: in be must kick-off their half own to prior All players.

7 **Number of players**: start if either seven game players A cannot team has than less.

8 **Duration of match**:

    a each 45 halves of game The in two minutes played consisting is.

    b minutes exceed 15 not must half The time interval.

9 **Fouls/misconduct**: equivalent Two cards one to are yellow red card.

10 **Free kicks**: A either direct be kick free can indirect or.

China and Football

Over two thousand years ago a football-type game known as *cuju*, or 'kick ball', was played in China. Players had to kick a ball through an opening in a net, and the use of hands wasn't allowed. A competitive form of the game was used as fitness training for the military. During the Han Dynasty (206 BC – AD 220), the popularity of *cuju* spread from the army to the royal courts and upper classes. It is said that the emperor Wu Di enjoyed the sport. Matches were often held inside the imperial palace. There are many ancient paintings and prints which depict games of *cuju* being played, both by men and women.

Fast-forward a couple of millenia and it is puzzling to many people how China, a nation of 1.35 billion inhabitants and with an excellent record in many other sporting spheres, is such a weak force in international football. The only time China qualified for the World Cup finals was in 2002, when they failed to score in any of their three matches. The team has never won a game at the Olympics. How come China can't produce a team of eleven players that can challenge the other mostly far smaller footballing nations?

Many theories have been put forward to explain this anomoly. One is that the Chinese authorities, while excellent at developing exceptional athletes and gymnasts to participate in mainly individualist disciplines, fail to see that the same methods don't apply so well to a team sport like football.

Another theory is that most Chinese parents expect their children to work really hard at school in order to get into university and hence have a higher chance of landing a good job. They see football as a waste of valuable studying time with no apparent future benefit, as the chances of becoming a top professional player are so remote.

Thirdly, corruption is rife at every level of the game in China: matches are regularly fixed, referees bribed, public money earmarked for new stadium construction ends up unaccounted for. In 2012, for example, Lu Jun, one of the country's most famous referees, was jailed for 5 and a half years for match-fixing. Two ex-heads of the football league were handed 10 and a half year sentences for corruption.

China's dismal record in international football is a question top officials in the Chinese government appear to have been mulling over in recent times. It was announced on 27 November 2014 that there are plans to have 20,000 special football schools throughout China by 2020, and 50,000 by 2025. Football is to become a compulsory part of the national curriculum at schools. It's encouraging for the success of this programme that President Xi Jingping is an enthusiastic follower of the game (as was the young Mao Zedong, who played as a goalkeeper at a teachers' college in his native Hunan Province).

While tens of millions of Chinese football fans passionately follow foreign leagues, in particular the Premier League, the Bundesliga, Serie A and La Liga, club football in China appears to be on the up. The China Super League was set up in 2004. Many famous foreign professionals – Robinho, Nicolas Anelka, Didier Drogba, Fredi Kanouté among others - have played for Super League sides. Top managers such as Marcello Lippi and Jean Tigana have coached some of its teams. The average attendance at CSL matches is around 19,000, only slightly lower than average crowds for fixtures in Italy's Serie A. Chinese club sides have twice won the Asian Champions League. Guangzhou were the most recent winners when they became champions in 2013.

If you had said to someone in 1965 that by 2015 China would have become the second biggest economy in the world, they probably wouldn't have believed you. Who knows, maybe in fifty years time people will view China the way we look at Brazil now, as the country most associated with the beautiful game.

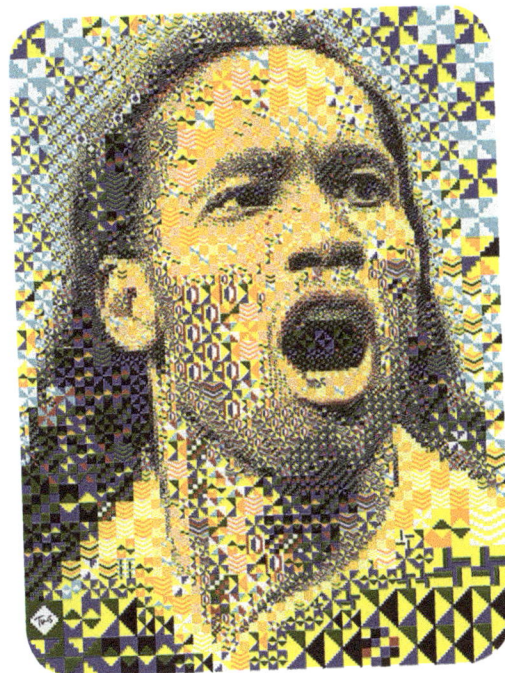

EXERCISE

Find the following in the text

1 An adjective meaning really bad. (paragraph 6)

2 An adjective meaning confusing. (para 2)

3 Another word for obligatory. (para 6)

4 A synonym of the verb to show. (para 1)

5 A verb meaning to get or acquire, especially when relating to jobs. (para 4)

6 An adjective meaning widespread or very common. (para 5)

7 A phrasal verb meaning to establish or found. (para 7)

8 A phrasal verb meaning to think deeply about something. (para 6)

9 A five-word phrase which means to be getting better, improving. (para 7)

10 A verb that means to conspire with others to arrange the score of a match. (para 5)

DISCUSSION

Do you think China will become a superpower of world football?

> " 'You owe me petrol money,' former Lech Poznań manager Franciszek Smuda told his coach, unimpressed by his advice to go and watch a young Robert Lewandowski playing. 'If **I'd wanted** to see trees, I would have gone to the forest instead. "

We use the past perfect to show clearly that one past event happened before another past event.

He lent her his season ticket	he forgot	now
_____*	_____*	_____* _____*

*He forgot that **he had lent** her his season ticket.*

This shows the chronology of events: first he lent his ticket, then later he forgot. Both events are in the past, but one (lending) happened before the other (forgetting).

Structure: Positive: had + past participle

Negative: hadn't + past participle

Question: Had…+ past participle

The contracted forms *I'd, he'd,* etc. and *hadn't* are used in speech and informal writing. The contraction of *had* is the same as the contraction of *would* - 'd -, but it's always clear from the context which one is intended.

Conjunctions such as *after, when, by the time* and *because* are often used to combine a past simple clause with a past perfect one.

*By the time Pelé retired in 1977, he **had achieved** what no other footballer **had ever achieved**: he **had won** the World Cup three times.*

We use the **past perfect simple** to talk about things that had already happened before the time we are talking about.

*There **had been** several accidents and dangerous incidents in stadiums before the Hillsborough disaster.*

We use the **past perfect continuous** to talk about longer actions or situations which had continued up to the past moment that we are talking about.

*Ronaldo **had been feeling** ill leading up to the 1998 World Cup final.*

Structure: Had + Been + -ing-form of the verb

We use it to focus on how long an activity continued or to focus on the activity itself.

*It wasn't a surprise when QPR were relegated as they'**d been struggling** for quite some time.*

*It was a shame when Theo Walcott got injured again as he'**d been linking** up really well with Cazorla and Sánchez.*

> ⚽ **DID YOU KNOW?** ⚽
>
> When Liverpool came back from being three goals down against AC Milan in the 2005 Champions League final, it was the first time in 112 years of existence that the club **had recovered** from three goals down.

The past perfect simple and continuous can be used to express disappointment or to talk about things that didn't turn out as expected.

*He'**d expected** to get his chance with the first team, but instead he was sent out on loan.*

*I'**d been hoping** to get some of the players' autographs, but they didn't hang around after the game, they went straight back on their coach.*

EXERCISE 👟

Complete the sentences with the *correct form* of the verbs in the box

leave	taunt	forget	expell	say	win	persuade
play	suffer	claim	fail	select	introduce	be able to

1 When José Mourinho returned to Barcelona as coach of Chelsea in 2005, he proclaimed that he _____ already _____ as many European Cups as Barça had in its history.

2 In June 1992, the FIFA congress readmitted South Africa to international football, the nation it _____ _____ from all international competition almost 30 years earlier.

3 When a 15 year old Samuel Eto'o arrived at a freezing Barajas airport dressed in shorts he found Madrid _____ _____ to send anybody there to meet him.

4 Edmundo was attacked by three Corinthians players who he _____ been _____, sparking a mass brawl.

5 The Chinese national team _____ _____ Korea 27 times but _____ never been _____ _____ beat them until they won 3-0 against them in the 2010 East Asia Football Championship.

6 Giancarlo Antognoni, a star of Italy's 1982 World Cup-winning team, _____ _____ a fractured skull in a league match that season, an injury which _____ _____ him in a coma for two days and that _____ almost _____ his life.

7 Italy drew their opening three games at Spain '82. No previous World Cup winners _____ ever _____ to win at least two of their opening three matches.

8 At the 1938 World Cup, Brazil manager Ademar Pimenta surprisingly dropped tournament top scorer Leônidas for their semi-final meeting with Italy. It was rumoured that associates of Mussolini _____ _____ Pimenta to leave the player out.

9 The Brazilian FA's preparation for the 1974 World Cup in Germany was meticulous. The squad all lived together for four months in a school outside Rio. Over this time, their chef _____ been gradually _____ West German ingredients and cooking fats to their meals. Their hotels in Germany _____ been _____ and booked in 1972.

10 Matthew Simmons, the fan who was famously on the receiving end of Eric Cantona's kung fu kick, claimed afterwards that all he _____ _____ was, 'An early bath for you, Cantona'.

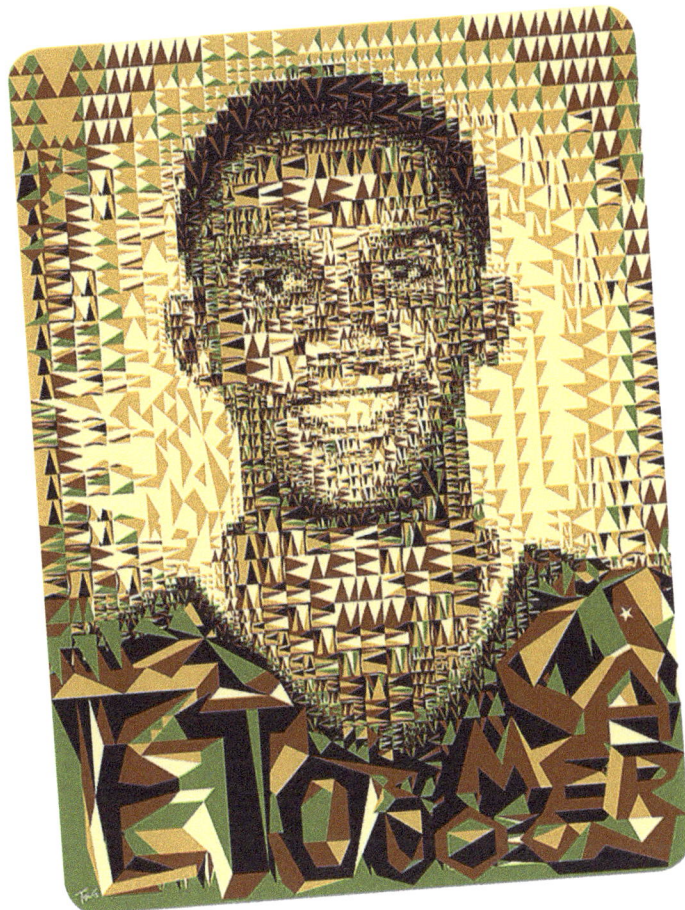

A League of their Own

A few years ago, some people in football _mooted_ the idea of an Atlantic League: a breakaway football competition involving some of the clubs in Northern and Western Europe that had possibly become too big for their own domestic leagues and that wanted the opportunity to compete against similar sides from around Europe, outside of the Champions League or the Europa League. It seems that the idea was _shelved_, but recently some involved in the game have raised the prospect once again. Today, we discuss the merits of such a concept with the football _think tank_, New Game.

Alain: I think it's an excellent idea. Especially regarding those clubs that completely dominate their own leagues, teams such as PSG and Celtic.

Bernardo: I agree. I wouldn't have it open to just the Northern and Western countries either, I'd invite the great Central European cities to come aboard. Think of the cities associated with the so-called Danubian school: Vienna, Budapest and Prague. How great would it be to have, say, Rapid Vienna, Honvéd and Sparta Prague involved!

Chris: Do you think the clubs we're talking about would want to leave their domestic leagues? That they'd be okay with drawing a line under their history and _starting from scratch_, as it were?

A: Well, take Celtic for example. Where's the fun in it when every title becomes a _procession_, year after year winning the Scottish league by 25 points or more? Imagine they were playing Benfica one week, Anderlecht the next, and after that FC Copenhagen.

C: Clubs which were great in the past but which have now fallen by the wayside, e.g. Honvéd, Leeds United, Hamburg, teams like this, could be revitalised and draw on their illustrious pasts to rise and be glorious again. New clubs in centres of strong football support, such as Dublin, could also be set up.

C: So how exactly do you _envisage_ the make-up of the league?

B: For me, there would be 18-20 clubs, all based in major cities. Let's see: Celtic or Rangers from Glasgow. Leeds, Newcastle or Sheffield Wednesday from England. Cardiff City. A _brand new_ mega club in Dublin playing out of their 50,000-seater national stadium. Lille, PSG or Lyon in France. Benfica and/or Porto. Valencia and/or Athletic Bilbao. Grasshoppers of Zürich. The 'Danubian' sides already mentioned. 1860 Munich, Hertha Berlin and/or Hamburg. FC Copenhagen, AIK in Stockholm. Ajax would be a massive _coup_, too, and PSV Eindhoven…

A: In fact, it was PSV's chairman and CEO, I think, who first put forward the idea for an Atlantic League. Anderlecht, too, maybe teams based in Helsinki and Oslo, and one or two from Northern Italy, say Torino, Genoa or Bologna. There has to be _scope_ for a huge club in Poland, too, even if, like in Dublin, there's no such club at present.

EUROMETRO

PanEuropa

LIGA STADT

C: That all sounds great. I really see it as a cosmopolitan, urban affair. In fact, I think that's what it should be called: the Cosmopolitan League. Or the CosmoEuro League, something like that. European cities were the _cradle_ of football, it seems appropriate to me to have a league like this. Would you not prefer to have Bayern Munich ahead of 1860?

B: I think some clubs might be too big for this league. I'm thinking Bayern, Barça, Real Madrid, Man Utd etc. There's every chance that they will form their own breakaway Super League anyway, there's been talk about it for years now, hasn't there?

A: Yes, there has. It's probable, in fact, that PSG would join such a league. In place of them, Racing Club de Paris could be re-established. I think one of the selling points of our new league would be the chance to break away from the _yoke_ of these mega clubs. I'd invite other clubs from Eastern Europe and the Balkans, too. Steaua Bucharest, Red Star Belgrade. Olympiakos and Panathinaikos in Greece, too.

C: What about League Euroville? _That has a certain ring to it_, doesn't it?

B: Or the Metropolitan League. Or MetroEuro?

C: But do you think fans of these clubs would be willing to leave their domestic leagues behind?

Some might not be. I do think, though, that if the league _took off_, the fans would get behind it, and other clubs would definitely want to join up. One could always start off with 10-12 clubs at first.

B: What about away support? The atmosphere in the stadiums would be _lacking_ if supporters didn't travel to matches.

A: All you really need is 1-2,000 away fans to create a nice little atmosphere, and it's so easy _nowadays_ to fly to other European cities.

B: These clubs could still compete in their domestic cup competitions, in order to retain a link with the past, if you like.

A: You could still maintain a system of promotion and relegation, too: the bottom few clubs could be replaced every year by the champions of their domestic leagues.

B: I'm not sure that relegation is really necessary. No-one minds that the same big clubs are in the Champions League season after season.

C: Would the domestic leagues not _be up in arms_ about this new tournament? I can see the breakaway clubs being branded as national traitors, abandoning their league for monetary gain.

B: There would definitely be considerable opposition. However, in time the domestic leagues might _come round to the idea_. Their own leagues would now be more competitive if the dominant club or clubs were gone, and they might also find that they can follow our new league _in tandem with_ their own, that they are separate entities.

C: What about UEFA, though? Would they _approve of_ it?

Probably not. I doubt they could stop it from happening, though.

They could _ban_ the clubs from entering the Champions League or the Europa League, or at least threaten to. However, I think if our league really took off, UEFA would want six or seven of our clubs in the Champions League, and others in the Europa. They'd be _cutting their nose off to spite their face_ if they didn't. I think our EuroMetro league could end up being the best league in Europe. 18-20 clubs, all with stadiums of 40,000-plus capacities. Think about it.

A: The league could financially support clubs at the start, to help them build or redevelop their stadiums. I think to talk about 40,000 capacities is understating the potential. Do you not think a club in Berlin could attract 80,000 fans if Dortmund can? Tottenham Hotspur have a 50,000-strong waiting list for season tickets. Based in the right urban centres, the potential of our league is enormous.

C: Its appeal is obvious, isn't it? I know if I was a Celtic fan I'd much rather be playing every week against Ajax, Benfica and Lyon than against Kilmarnock, Falkirk and Partick Thistle, that's for sure.

A: When you think about how much the Poles, the Swedes, the Irish and the Danes love their football, I really think each of these nations could have one super club which the whole country effectively could _get behind_. The atmosphere around games would be more like the atmosphere at the Euros than at the Champions League. Wouldn't it be great to see the Danish Roligans out in force!

B: There are lots of other candidates too: Marseille, Aston Villa, Sevilla, Fiorentina. It'd be great to include Dynamo Kiev as well, it's a massive club.

A: Regarding a club having to draw a line under its history and start again from scratch, this is an _exaggeration_. Competitions come and go. No-one talks about the Mitropa Cup, the Fairs Cup or the Cup Winners Cup any more, but you'll still see the cups on display in club museums and trophy rooms. Starting up new tournaments doesn't mean that clubs' entire histories are _wiped out._

B: True. I can see a scenario where the top six teams from our new league play the top six from a breakaway Super League in a separate competition, which could even replace the Champions League.

C: We really need to think up a name. The Continental League? The PanEuropa? TransEurope League?

A: Stadt Liga, or Liga Stadt? The Inter-City?

B: The Continent? The Europeira? You know what, it'll probably end up being named after its main _sponsor_, won't it?

EXERCISE 👟

Find the underlined words or phrases in the text which mean the following

1 To officially or legally prohibit something.

2 To back, to support.

3 A group of intellectuals providing advice and ideas on specific political or economic problems.

4 Suggested or put forward an idea.

5 These days (in contrast with the past).

6 Deficient in something.

7 A person or organisation that supports someone financially.

8 To agree as satisfactory, to think something is a good idea.

9 Punishing someone, but by punishing them, you hurt yourself, too.

10 Completely erased.

11 To be really angry about something.

12 To recommence from the very start.

13 (An idea or a plan) put to one side for the moment.

14 Room, possibility.

15 An over-statement of something.

16 A formality.

17 At the same time as, alongside.

18 Became successful.

19 To picture, imagine.

20 A type of furniture in which a baby sleeps, a place where something is born or develops.

21 To gradually accept an idea or suggestion.

22 People who are disloyal.

23 That sounds good.

24 Perfectly new.

25 A significant achievement in the pursuit of a goal.

26 The oppressive burden.

DISCUSSION

Do you think the Atlantic League is a good idea?

Will the top clubs set up a breakaway Super League?

Do you think they should?

'Will' for the Future

> At 28, Eric Cantona is exactly as he was at 18 and as he **will be** at 38 – violent, rebellious, heroic and shipwrecked.

—L'ÉQUIPE

Positive:	will +verb	'We'll beat them'
Negative:	will not (won't) + verb	'We won't beat them'
Question:	Will …+verb?	'Will we beat them?'

We use *will* to talk about

1 Decisions at the time of speaking.

*I'm heading. This match is over.' 'Wait, **I'll come** with you.'*

2 Predictions, often with *believe, expect, hope, doubt, be sure* and *think*.

*I think AC Milan **will come back** to be a major force in European football again.*

3 Offers

***Will you have** another pint? Ah, go on.*

4 Willingness

***I'll lend** you my season ticket if I'm not going to the game.*

5 Refusal

*He just **won't pass** the ball, he's so selfish.*

6 Requests.

***Will you remind** me to record the Champions League highlights programme later?*

7 Firm intentions and promises.

*Deportivo la Coruna are my team and **I'll support** them through thick and thin.*

***I won't tell** you the score. I promise!*

8 Threats.

***You'll be** sorry you said that!*

9 Facts about the future.

*The Ballon d'Or ceremony **will be held** next month in Switzerland.*

10 To talk about future events we haven't arranged yet.

***We'll probably leave** our house in the early afternoon.*

11 Habits

***He'll** happily **spend** all day Sunday watching football: English, Spanish, German, whatever is on.*

12 Tendencies

*New players **will** often **start off** really strongly only for their form to dip a couple of months into a season.*

The difference between *going to* and *will* for predictions

Going to is used more for observations when you have outside evidence for what you say.

*Agh, that's a terrible tackle and he's already been booked. **He's going to** get sent off.*

Will is used to talk about what we believe or have calculated, often based on our past experience or opinions.

*I believe **there will be** a European Super League in the not-too-distant future. I could see Madrid, Barça, PSG, Juve, Man Utd, Man City, Chelsea and a few others forming their own competition.*

Will is also used in the 1st conditional:

*If it snows again this afternoon, the match **will be** suspended.*

EXERCISE

Complete the sentences with a verb from the box

be	speak	be	boo	win	play	pay
be able	come on	sing	top	be	overcome	

1 'Give me ten pieces of wood and Zinedine Zidane and I'll _____ you the Champions League.' –Alex Ferguson

2 'I have won many trophies in my time, but nothing will ever _____ helping win the battle for peace in my country.' – Didier Drogba

3 Supporters can be very fickle: one week they'll _____ their love for a player, the next week they'll _____ him off the pitch.

4 Italian teams will often _____ defensively for 70 minutes and then try to catch their opponents on the break.

5 'You, players, will soon _____ hailed as champions by millions of your compatriots. You Brazilians have no rivals in the entire hemisphere. You will _____ any opponent. I salute you already as the winners.' - Ângelo Mendes de Moraes, mayor of Rio, shortly before kick-off of the final game, Brazil v Uruguay, of the 1950 World Cup. Uruguay won 2-1, becoming World Champions.

6 'There's no compassion among professionals,' Harald Schumacher said after his appalling challenge on Patrick Battiston in the 1982 World Cup semi-final which left Battiston unconscious. On hearing that the Frenchman had lost two teeth, he added, 'Tell him I'll _____ for the crowns.'

7 'I will _____ _____ as a substitute and score in the last ten minutes,' predicted Dutch player Dick Nanninga before the 1978 World Cup final. He scored a header eight minutes from time to equalise for Holland, having been brought on shortly before this.

8 The final week of the 1990 World Cup, which was won by West Germany, coincided with the reunification of Germany. The winning manager, Franz Beckenbauer, was quoted as saying: 'I'm sorry for the other countries, but now that we will _____ _____ to incorporate all the great players from the East, the German team will _____ unbeatable for a long time to come.'

9 'I will not _____ to cheating bastards.' - Brian Clough refuses to talk to the Turin press, after his team Derby County lost to Juventus in the semi-final of the 1973 European Cup.

10 'No colour will ever _____ brighter for me than black or white.' – Alessandro Del Piero, proud to wear the Juventus shirt.

Random Football Tales

In 2008, Argentine forward Adrián Bastía was sent off for tripping a pitch invader during a Greek league game in Athens. No doubt he thought he was doing the right thing when he tackled the supporter, but this is not how the referee saw it: the Asteras Tripolis player was shown a straight red card for violent conduct.

Before the start of the 1970 World Cup final between Brazil and Italy, Pelé drew the referee's attention to a problem with his boot. When Pelé bent down to tie his lace, the TV cameras zoomed in, so millions of viewers around the world could see that he was wearing a pair of Puma boots. It later emerged that Pelé had been offered $120,000 by the sportswear company to draw attention to his footwear.

Jan van Beveren, the great Dutch goalkeeper, who boycotted his national team and so missed the 1974 World Cup, became a stamp dealer in Dallas after he retired from football.

Many footballers have odd rituals and superstitious habits. Bobby Moore, England's 1966 World Cup-winning captain, refused to put his shorts on before the rest of his England team-mates. As a joke, Martin Peters, one of his team-mates, would sometimes take his shorts back off after Moore had put his on, which meant that Moore would have to take his shorts off again and wait until Peters put his back on.

Ronaldinho first came to media attention when his youth team won a game 23-0. He scored every single goal.

Alfredo Di Stéfano was kidnapped in Caracas when he was on a pre-season tour of South America with Real Madrid. On the night of 24 August 1963, the star was abducted from his hotel by the Venezuelan revolutionary group known as FALN. He was released unharmed two days later close to the Spanish embassy, even playing a match against São Paulo FC the following day. A Spanish film called *Real, La Película* based on the story of the kidnapping was released in 2005. In a bizarre publicity stunt at the premiere, kidnapper Paul de Rio, who was by now a famous artist, and Di Stéfano were brought together for the first time since the abduction 41 years earlier.

Polonia Warsaw is one of eastern Europe's most romantic clubs. It was founded by the Warsaw intelligentsia. Many of its players fought in the Warsaw Uprising of 1944. It has always counted artists, scientists and writers among its fans.

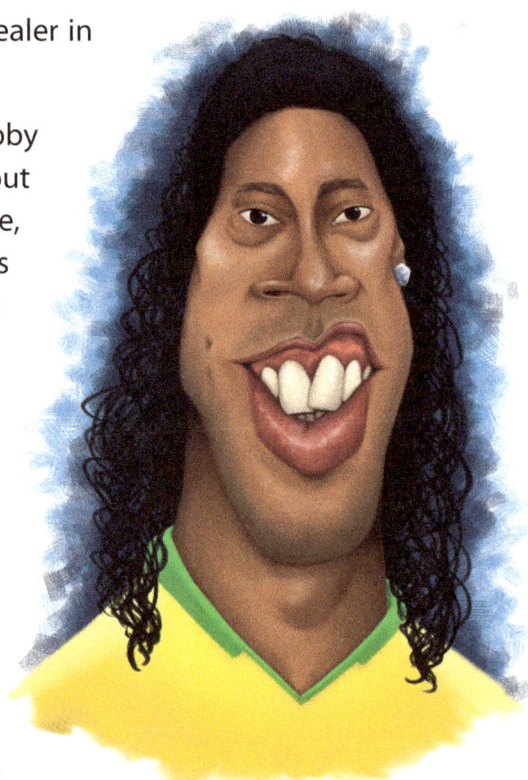

Slovakia player Peter Dubovský, who played for Slovan Bratislava, Real Madrid and Oviedo, fell to his death taking pictures of a waterfall in the Thai resort of Ko Samui. He was just 28.

The longest move that has led to a goal was a 35-pass move that ended with Nicolas Anelka scoring for Fenerbahçe in an Istanbul derby with Galatasary. The move involved every outfield player.

The first goal ever scored in the English Football League was an own goal. It was scored by Aston Villa defender Gershom Cox in their game against Wolverhampton Wanderers, on 8 September 1888.

Some believe it an advantage for footballers to have small feet. Lothar Matthäus, Gheorghe Hagi, Sócrates (who was 6'3") and Hristo Stoichkov all wore size five boots. Messi, on the other hand, wears size 8.5 (UK). The Nigerian Kanu had size fifteen feet.

In 1977, Luciano Re Cecconi, an important player on Lazio's Scudetto-winning team of 1974, and a friend went into a local jewellery shop. Bruno Tabocchini, the proprietor, had recently been the victim of two armed robberies. Re Cecconi knew of Tabocchini's misfortune. He was used to playing practical jokes with his friends and team-mates, and pretending to have a gun under his jacket, he called out: 'everyone stop, this is a robbery'. The shocked jeweller did not recognise the player and reacted by shooting him in the chest. Re Cecconi died shortly after. Tabocchini was arrested but never convicted of any crime.

When Walther Bensemann was just 14, he founded Montreux F.C. He helped found Karlsruher FV when he was just 18. He was also involved in the creation of Frankfurter Kickers, which would later become Eintracht Frankfurt. In 1920, he founded *Kicker* which to this day is Germany's leading football magazine. In 1933, he was forced to leave Germany because of the political situation. He died soon after in Montreux in relative obscurity.

Johann Cruyff lost everything he owned when an unscrupulous business partner persuaded him to invest all his money – some $2.4 million – in a disastrous pig-breeding venture in Spain.

Footballers will make good businessmen someday – well, someday when pigs fly.

You made a right pig's ear of that, didn't you?

You were really sold a pig in a poke.

*

Mark each statement either *true* **or** *false* **according to the text**

1 Johann Cruyff's pig-breeding business was a success.

2 Some Polonia Warsaw players took part in the Warsaw Uprising of 1944.

3 Ronaldinho once scored 23 goals in one game.

4 Jan van Beveren became an art dealer when he retired from football.

5 Pelé didn't really have a problem with his boot before the 1970 World Cup final.

6 When Gersham Cox scored the first ever goal in the English Football League, Wolves took a one goal lead against Aston Villa.

7 Messi wears size 9 shoes.

8 Nicolas Anelka scored a goal for Galatasaray at the end of a 35-pass move.

9 Walther Bensemann founded Kicker magazine.

10 Luciano ReCecconi planned to steal jewellery from the shop.

---

* *When pigs fly* is a way of saying that something will never happen. It's used for humorous effect, to laugh at over-ambition.

A pig in a poke is something that is bought or accepted without first being seen or assessed.

To *make a pig's ear of something* means to do something badly, wrongly or awkwardly.

Future Continuous and Future Perfect

Future Continuous – shall/will + be + -ing

We use the future continuous to

1   Refer to routine things.

*I'**ll be going** by bus as usual.*

It emphasises that no new arrangement is necessary.

*I can give you a lift to the stadium – I'**ll be going** that way anyway.*

2   Ask about someone's plans. The future continuous is more polite than the future simple.

*Where **will** you **be staying** when you go to Paris?*

3   Talk about an activity that has already been decided.

*The England squad **will be staying** at the Caipirinha Hotel, located in a quiet suburb of Rio.*

4   Describe or predict events or situations continuing at a particular point in the future or over a period of time in the future.

*This time next week, all our players **will be lying** on a beach somewhere hot and enjoying their holidays.*

*I'm sure our scouts **will be watching** the forthcoming U-17 World Cup closely to see if they can find any stars of the future.*

Future Perfect (simple) – shall/will have + past participle

We use the future perfect simple to talk about a future event that will finish before or at a specified time in the future, often with *before, by + a fixed time* or *in + an amount of time.*

*'In a week's time, the World Cup **will have finished** and we will know who the winner is.'*

We also use it in the first conditional.

If Messi spends the rest of his career at Barça,
*he **will have** only ever **played** for one club at senior level.*

Future Perfect (continuous) – shall/will have + been +-ing

We use the future perfect continuous to show how long an activity or situation has been in progress before a specified time in the future. We usually mention the length of time.

*He **will have been sitting** on the bench for the whole season if the manager doesn't play him in in our final game next week.*

EXERCISE 👟

Complete the following predictions with the correct words

won	become	travelling	waiting	playing	broken
won	playing	hosted	earning	banned	

In 25 years time…

1 Clubs such as PSG, Celtic, Ajax, Porto and FC Copenhagen - teams that dominate their domestic leagues - will have _____ away from their home leagues to form a new Europe-wide league tournament, in competition with the Champions League.

2 People will be _____ more to watch games in foreign leagues.

3 Football, i.e. soccer, will have _____ the most popular sport in the United States.

4 England will have _____ the World Cup again.

5 Some teams will be _____ behind closed doors, as their fans will have been _____ for hooliganism.

6 The top players will be _____ a million euros per week.

7 China will have _____ the World Cup.

8 Liverpool supporters will have been _____ 50 years for a league title.

9 Barcelona will have _____ more Champions League/European Cup titles than Real Madrid.

10 Due to advancements in science, more players will be _____ into their forties.

DISCUSSION 🔔

Which of the above predictions do you think will come true?

Make your own predictions about the future of the game.

Celebrations Gone Wrong

Players often say that scoring a goal is the greatest feeling in the world. However, this ecstasy can quickly turn to agony if the player loses control of himself during his goal celebration. Here are some examples of when celebrations went wrong.

Who can forget the sight of Ole Gunnar Solskjær scoring the dramatic winning goal for Man Utd in the 1999 Champions League final? Unfortunately for him, his sliding celebration resulted in him tearing his medial ligament.

Shortly after signing for Chelsea in 1999, Celestine Babayaro broke his leg while celebrating a goal with his trademark somersault in a pre-season friendly against Stevenage. He couldn't make his league debut for his new club until months later.

Martin Palermo's La Liga career with Villarreal was cut short when the Argentine player celebrated a goal in 2002. He climbed onto a small wall behind the goal, supporters piled down to join in the celebration, and all this caused the fragile wall to collapse. He suffered a double knee fracture and never fully recovered his best form, eventually moving back to Boca Juniors in 2004 via short spells at Real Betis and Alavés. (Unlucky Palermo is also in the record books for being the only player ever to miss three penalties in a single international match; he fluffed his lines three times from the spot for Argentina in a Copa América tie with Colombia. More happily, though, he is Boca Junior's all-time top goalscorer with 236 goals to his name.)

Servette Geneva midfielder Paulo Diogo ripped off the top of his finger when his wedding ring got caught in the perimeter fence as he celebrated a Swiss league goal with supporters in 2004. Play was held up to search for the finger and, to add insult to injury (literally), he was booked for time-wasting. (Now you know why it's a good thing that referees and their assistants check that players aren't wearing jewellery when they come on to the pitch.)

Fabián Espindola sprained an ankle while performing a somersault celebration for Real Salt Lake City in 2008 which sidelined him for two months. The goal itself was disallowed.

In September 2014, Coritiba forward Joel leapt the advertising hoardings behind the goal, unaware that there was an opening with steps leading down from the pitch to the dressing rooms which was only covered by a large Coritiba flag. One of the stewards tried to warn Joel against making the jump, but the player couldn't hear him because of the noise in the stadium. The forward, who was helped out of the ditch by stadium officials and team-mates, escaped with a minor injury and was able to continue the match.

The most awful case happened in India in October 2014. 23-year-old Peter Biaksangzuala died from severe spinal cord damage suffered when attempting to celebrate a goal with a somersault. The Bethlehem Vengthlang FC midfielder died at a hospital in the northeastern Indian state of Mizoram after the incident in a third-tier Mizoram Premier League (MPL) match.

EXERCISE

Say whether the following statements are *true* or *false*

1   Joel was playing for Corinthians when he fell down the hole in the ground.

2   The referee ruled out Fabián Espindola's goal.

3   Martin Palermo never played football again after his double leg fracture.

4   Peter Biaksangzuala died instantly when he damaged his spinal cord.

5   Paolo Diogo was shown a yellow card for time-wasting.

6   No-one has scored more goals for Boca Juniors than Martin Palermo.

7   Ole Gunnar Solskjær scored the winner in the 1999 Cup Winners Cup final.

> " If **you have** a Ferrari and **I have** a small car, to beat you in a race, **I have to break** your wheel or **put** sugar in your tank. "

–JOSÉ MOURINHO

Zero Conditional

if + present tense, + present tense

OR

present tense + if + present tense

We use the Zero Conditional to talk about something that is a fact or a general truth or always happens as a result of something else. You can use the present simple, continuous, perfect or passive in either clause.

*A game **goes** to a penalty shoot-out if the sides **are** level after extra time.*

When the *if* clause comes first in a sentence, it is followed by a comma.

Note: we can use the past tense if we're talking about something we know or believed happened or was true. It's the zero conditional in the past.

*If it **rained**, our fathers **drove** us to training.*

⚽ **DID YOU KNOW?** ⚽

If a corner flag **is broken** and **cannot be repaired** or **replaced**, the referee **has to abandon** the game.

First Conditional

We use the First Conditional to talk about something we feel is a probable future result. You can use any present tense in the *if* clause and any future form, imperative or some modal verbs in the other clause.

Conditional clause	Main clause
If + present simple	modal verb
If you want	you can come with us.
If + present simple	be going to (future)
If we keep up this pressure	we're going to score soon.
If + present simple	imperative
If you can't find your seat	ask a steward.
If + present continuous	will + bare infinitive
If you're planning to go to the away game	I'll come with you.
If + present perfect	will + bare infinitive
If they've concluded negotiations	he'll be able to play on Saturday.
If + present perfect	modal verb
If he's said he's not happy here	they should let him talk to other clubs.
Imperative	and/or + will
Try your best	and you'll get what you deserve.

There are some alternatives to *if*. *Unless* is the most important one. It means *if not*. There's no important difference between *if* and *unless*.

> *Unless you train hard, you won't become a top professional player.*

> *If you don't train hard, you won't become a top professional player.*

Whether is another alternative to *if*. We can also use *as/so long as, on condition (that), provided/ providing (that), in case, suppose/supposing (that)* to introduce conditional clauses.

Compare the First and Second Conditionals (see the unit Unreal Conditionals)

1st: *If they hire a new manager, the players will have to try to impress him. (= I think there is a possibility that the club will hire a new manager.)*

2nd: *If they hired a new manager, the players would have to try to impress him. (= I don't really think the club are going to hire a new manager, I'm just speculating.)*

EXERCISE

Put the words in the box in the correct form to complete the sentences

be	shoot	be	go	discuss	hope	have	be	score	know

1 'If there _____ a sequence of 15 previous passes, a good transition between attack and defence is impossible. Impossible.' – Pep Guardiola

2 A game cannot continue if one side _____ reduced to six players.

3 Unless you _____ someone at the club, you'll never get a job there.

4 'If you don't _____, you won't score.' – 1954 World Cup-winning German manager Sepp Herberger, known for his simple, but wise, sayings.

5 'If I _____ against Liverpool, I will not celebrate.' – Fernando Torres, returning to play at Anfield.

6 Before signing for them in 1966, Velibor Vasović watched Ajax play a home game against PSV. A 17-year-old Cruyff was playing on the left wing. Vasović was told that the club's best player, Piet Keizer, normally played on the left wing. 'You can tell the president if they _____ anyone better than this player (Cruyff), they don't need me,' he said.

7 'If Ryan Giggs _____ worth £20 million, Dennis Bergkamp is worth £100 million.' – Marco van Basten

8 'If we are going to get knocked out playing like that, then I _____ our plane crashes on the way home.' - Argentina manager Bilardo after his team's loss to Cameroon at Italia '90.

9 'He has to get his two cents in even if we're only _____ the menu.' – former assistant coach of Germany Erich Ribbeck on Lothar Matthäus.

10 'If you're _____ to get run over, it's better if it's a Rolls-Royce that does it.' - Johan Cruyff, speaking after his Barcelona team lost to an impressive São Paulo side in the 1992 Intercontinental Cup.

14 legend

Jumbled-up Words: What's my Injury?

Rearrange the letters in the following words to form common injuries suffered by footballers. The first letter in each word is done for you

e.g. **S**rpnidea **a**eknl

answer: Sprained ankle

1 **T**ron **h**gnatsirm

2 **B**kneor **m**lettaarsa

3 **D**dae **l**ge

4 **D**edcatolsi **s**udlhore

5 **T**nor **a**sellchi **t**nnedo

6 **P**dlleu **t**ghhi **m**sclue

7 **F**catrdure **c**keeh **b**eno

8 **C**noiscusno

9 **G**noir **s**nrtai

10 **R**dertuup **l**iagstmen

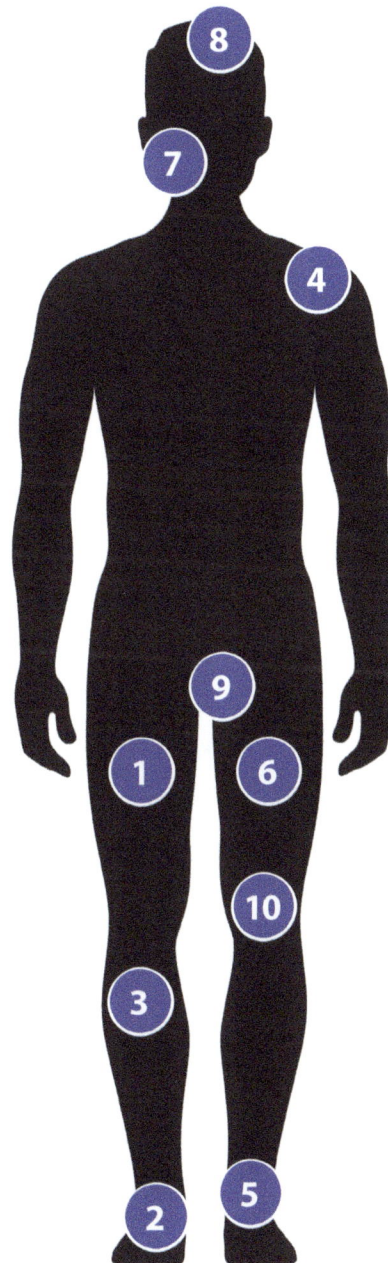

Football on Film

Television arts programme host Aldo Mancini and three guests are discussing some football films they have all watched.

Aldo: So, first up for discussion is *The Goalkeeper's Anxiety at the Penalty Kick*, a film by Wim Wenders. Claudio, what were your impressions?

Claudio: Well, to be honest, I found it quite hard _to get into_ this film. I thought it was quite _ponderous_ and slow-moving at times. Probably a bit too _arty_ for my taste. There were some good things about it – they way it was shot, and some of the acting was excellent – but overall, I'm sorry to say I thought it a bore. And I'd consider myself a fan of Wim Wenders, I'd like to add.

Kirsten: Really? I thought it had a great tension to it. We were really made to feel like we were in the goalie's shoes. Or at least that's what I felt anyway. I thought Arthur Brauss's performance was particularly strong. I'd describe it as a gripping psychological thriller.

Julie: I fell asleep during it.

Kirsten: Oh come on! I think you should give it another chance. It rewards watching it the whole way through.

Aldo: Okay, next up we have *Escape to Victory*. It's a story about a group of Allied prisoners in the Second World War who _take on_ their guards in a football match and plan to escape during the half-time interval. Kirsten, what did you think of it?

Kirsten: I liked it, it was exciting. The acting was strong, and the live football action scenes were credible. Apart from maybe Sylvester Stallone's save towards the end of the film. Oh dear, haha!

Claudio: I struggled _to suspend my disbelief_, to be honest. I mean, Michael Caine, Pelé and Sylvester Stallone in the same film, not to mention most of the Ipswich Town squad from the early 1980s? Seriously?

Julie: I think it's one of those films that you need to see at least once, it's so well-known. I thought Pelé was quite good in it, actually. There's enough tension in the movie to keep you interested.

Aldo: The next film we watched was *Looking for Eric*. Who'd like to start?

Claudio: I loved this one. It was funnier than I thought it would be. _Edgier_ too - there was darkness that I wasn't expecting.

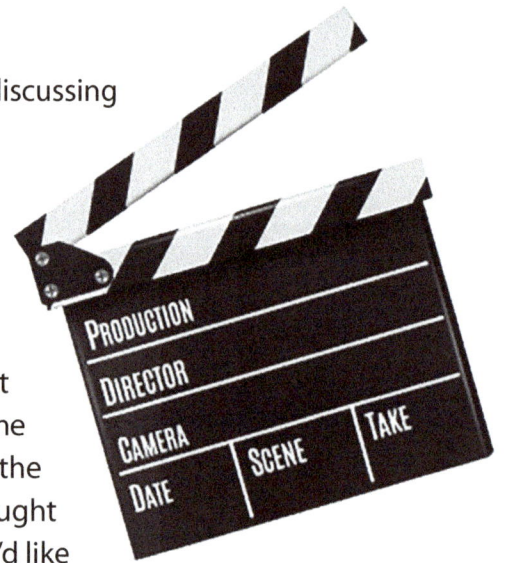

Kirsten: I agree. Do you think Eric Cantona is really as he is portrayed in the film, or is he kind of playing up to his image in a mock-theatrical kind of way?

Claudio: Well, I think that is how he speaks, but the philosophical asides are an _in-joke_ reference to some of his interviews at press conferences; most famously when he spoke about the seagulls following the _trawler_.

Julie: Agreed. There were a few interesting _sub-plots_, too. For example, they showed the tension between the fans of big clubs like Man Utd and those fans, or former fans, who are rebelling against the commercialisation of the game and have set up FC United of Manchester.

Kirsten: Cantona comes across as a charismatic and likeable guy, doesn't he?

Claudio: Yes, he does. I thought the leading actor was a good _foil_ for him. He's kind of timid, beaten down by life, but finds inner strength that he didn't know he had.

Kirsten: It is an enjoyable watch, isn't it? Ken Loach is a reliable director. This certainly isn't as _grim_ as some of his films can be.

Aldo: So, the next film we're going to discuss is _The Miracle of Berne_, which is based around the true story of West Germany's surprising victory in the 1954 World Cup in Switzerland.

Julie: I loved this movie and will definitely watch it again some time. It was beautifully _shot_ and the acting was excellent.

Claudio: Agreed. There are some nice touches of humour, too. The German manager, Sepp Herberger, was _renowned_ for his often tongue-in-cheek, pithy little pearls of wisdom, e.g. 'The ball is round', and 'A game lasts 90 minutes'. We see him in the film saying some of these at press conferences.

Kirsten: It's really a film about how Germany _came to terms with_ its defeat in the Second World War. The father returning after having spent years in a Russian prison is a very powerful device to employ.

Claudio: It's notoriously tricky to convincingly _portray_ live football action on film, but I think the director of this movie did a very good job.

Aldo: Okay, moving swiftly on to our next film, which is _Africa United_, a film about five African kids who travel 3,000 miles across the continent to try to get to the World Cup in South Africa. Julie, your reaction, please.

Julie: Oh this was _touching_, wasn't it? It's visually great, too – you get all the _vivid_ primary colours of Africa. I'd grown so _fond_ of all five of the kids by the end of the movie.

Kirsten: I thought Dudu was hilarious. His animated fantasy sequences were really well done, both funny and surreal. Credit to the creative people behind them. On the DVD extras they show how they shot some of these sequences, which is fascinating.

Claudio: I thought at times they overdid his _malapropisms_, but maybe I'm being a bit _nit-picky_. I liked the film a lot. I was afraid that it was going to be a bit twee, but it was actually pretty hard-hitting in places. I mean, they managed to tackle tricky subjects like AIDS, prostitution and gun violence in what is essentially a light enough family comedy.

Kirsten: I loved the soundtrack, too.

Aldo: Right, so, our last film was _Rudo y Cursi_. This is about two Mexican half-brothers who live on a banana plantation. One day, an agent sees them playing football and offers to take one of them on trial. They both end up playing professionally in Mexico City.

Julie: I saw this as a film about how hard it is for someone from an under-priviledged background to survive in the world of professional football.

Claudio: I agree. It's not really a film about football so much as it's a film about two brothers _striving_ to provide better lives for themselves and their families.

Kirsten: Well, there's still quite a lot of football in there too, though, isn't there? It was a good portrayal of how the game is surrounded by many _shady_ characters. I also found it very funny at times: I laughed out loud on several occasions.

Aldo: Yes, the _sibling rivalry_ between the two main protagonists is amusing. There were some surprising twists and turns in the storline, too, weren't there? I thought some of the cinematography was lovely as well.

Julie: It shows how hypocritical and hyper-critical supporters can be, doesn't it?

Claudio: True, it really does.

EXERCISE

Find the underlined words or phrases in the text which mean the following

1   Describing a film not aimed at the mainstream.

2   Affectionate.

3   To deal with or come to accept.

4   To show.

5   The secondary storylines in a book, play or film.

6   The mistaken use of a word in place of a similar-sounding one, often with an amusing effect.

7 Type of fishing boat.

8 To start to enjoy a book or film etc.

9 A person or thing that contrasts with and so emphasises and enhances the qualities of another.

10 Very bright, intense.

11 Jokes that only a few people in a group understand.

12 Slow-moving, laboured.

13 To try to put your normal critical faculties to one side in order to enjoy an unrealistic film or book, etc.

14 Affecting you emotionally.

15 To challenge or confront.

16 To be known or celebrated for.

17 Sinister, disreputable.

18 Bleak, depressing.

19 Grittier, not so pretty or nice.

20 Too critical of minor details or trivial matters.

21 The competitiveness between brothers and sisters.

22 Trying really hard to achieve something.

23 Filmed.

DISCUSSION

Which of the films discussed in the article have you seen?

Which would you like to see?

Unreal Conditionals

> **If** God **had wanted** us to play football in the sky,
> **he'd have put** grass up there.

–BRIAN CLOUGH, NOTTINGHAM FOREST'S EUROPEAN CUP-WINNING MANAGER,
NOT A FAN OF THE LONG-BALL GAME.

If the situation is unreal (imaginary or very improbable), we show this by backshifting the verb.

*If we signed two or three top class players,
we would be in a position to challenge for the title.*

In the above sentence, we are talking about the present or the future, but we use the past tense *signed* to show that signing these players is improbable or hypothetical, i.e. you are just imagining or speculating about this.

In the second clause of the sentence we generally use *would*. We can also use *might* or *maybe* for possible results.

Second Conditional (unreal/improbable in the present or the future)

if + past simple, would + verb

*If I **had** the time and money, I **would try** to go
and see a game at every club in Germany.*

Third Conditional (unreal in the past/imagining how a situation or event might have been different in the past).

If + past perfect, would + present perfect

*If we **had signed** two or three top class players a few seasons ago,
we **would have qualified** for the Champions League by now.*

In the above sentence, we are talking about the past, and imagining how things would have been different if certain events had happened .

48 • LEARN ENGLISH THROUGH FOOTBALL

Sometimes we make sentences which mix the second and third conditionals, especially when a past event has an effect on the present.

*Would Messi **be** such a great player if he **hadn't undergone** growth hormone treatment?*

*'If football **was** a drug, I **would have died** from overdose.' – Fernando Torres*

EXERCISE 👟

Complete the sentences using the words in the box

might	complained	take	been	done	gave	tried	have
played	would	could	had	couldn't	become	score	

1   'Only a madman would _____ children to a football game in Italy' – Massimiliano Allegri, April 2015, after violence erupted between Juventus and Torino supporters.

2   'We got a title, but what was it in relation to this sadness? If I _____ play the match again, I would _____ against us.' – Obdulio Varela, captain of the Uruguay team that beat Brazil in the final game of the 1950 World Cup, the famous 'Maracanazo'.

3   'I don't think you can blame Henry,' said Republic of Ireland winger Damien Duff after the infamous Thierry Henry double handball incident when France played Ireland in a play-off in 2009. 'If it was myself or Robbie (Keane) down the other end, we would have _____ it.'

4   'Without the Surinamese, Dutch football would have _____ a little more like German football.' – Humberto Tan, Dutch journalist.

5   'As a coach, my teams _____ have won more games if we'd _____ in a less adventurous way. Maybe I'd _____ earned a little more and the bonuses would have _____ bigger, but if people say that Barcelona were playing the nicest football in the world with me as coach, what more can I ask for?' – Johann Cruyff

6   'If you shut them up in a room by themselves, they _____ even write home a letter to mother.' – César Luis Menotti, former Argentina manager, talking about journalists.

7 'I'm sure we wouldn't have _____ if an English player had scored that way.' – Bobby Robson, England manager at the 1986 World Cup, referring to Maradona's infamous goal.

8 'I'm sure the England selectors thought if they _____ me the job, I'd want to run the show. They were shrewd because that's exactly what I would have _____.' – Brian Clough on why he never became England manager.

9 'If Barcelona _____ Liverpool's fans, or Arsenal's, or United's, we'd have won 20 Champions Leagues.' – Xavi

10 Before he joined River Plate's youth academy, Radamel Falcao had begun journalism studies, so if he hadn't become a footballer, he _____ have been a writer.

What springs to mind when you think of France and football? An elegantly dishevelled Michel Platini winding his way through opposition defences? Great clubs like Olympique de Marseille, Paris Saint-Germain and Lyon? Or maybe you can visualise beret-wearing supporters lustily singing La Marseillaise? The cockerel? *L'Équipe* newspaper? Zinedine Zidane's headbutt, Thierry Henry's handball?

L'ÉQUIPE

In fact, French involvement in, and influence on, European and world football is more profound than many people are aware of. FIFA, UEFA, the European and UEFA Cups, and the European Championship and the World Cup were all ideas dreamt up and brought to fruition by Frenchmen.

In 1903, Frenchman **Robert Guérin**, a journalist for Le Matin newspaper, set up the Federation International de Football Association, which is now known by its acronym FIFA. He initially invited representatives of the major European football federations to a meeting held in Paris, where Holland, Belgium, Switzerland, Denmark, Spain and Sweden all joined up. Guérin was elected president at the inaugral Congress, remaining in the post for two years. The English, who at the time were quite xenophobic, at least when it came to international football, would become FIFA members in 1905. Over the following years the association expanded internationally. Today, it has more members than the United Nations.

Jules Rimet was president of FIFA from 1921 until 1954. He was one of the pivotal figures behind the creation of the football World Cup. He awarded Uruguay the honour of staging the first World Cup and commissioned a golden trophy which was later renamed in his honour. His efforts in establishing the global tournament led to him being nominated for the Nobel Peace Prize in 1956.

FIFA®

Henri Delaunay was general secretary of the French Football Federation from its foundation in 1919. He sat on the board of FIFA from 1924 until 1928, and along with Jules Rimet, was an early architect of the World Cup. In 1927, he attended the meeting in Zürich where several of the masterminds of international football got together to discuss a global tournament. It was Delaunay who strongly advocated opening the competition to FIFA members worldwide, and to hold the event every 4 years.

He was a pivotal figure in the founding of UEFA, an organisation set up in response to the weakening power European members felt they had over FIFA, and he was general secretary from its foundation on 15 June 1954 until his death in 1955. Delaunay wrote a key essay, 'Is it possible to build a footballing Europe?'.

He was largely responsible for the creation of the European Championship, the trophy which is named after him, having first proposed the idea of a pan-European competition as far back as 1927. The first tournament was held in 1960, three years after his death. He was succeeded as head of UEFA by his son **Pierre**.

The European Champion Clubs' Cup was an idea born in the summer of 1955 in the offices of the French daily sports newspaper *L'Équipe* and was dreamed up by its football correspondent and editor **Gabriel Hanot** and his colleague **Jacques Ferran**.

He was inspired by the Mitropa Cup, the central European club tournament set up by Hugo Meisl before the Second World War.

In June 1955, the 65-year-old Hanot handed over his vision to UEFA who named it the European Champion Clubs' Cup, but it was always more popularly known as the European Cup. The inaugral tournament was a great success, proving that Hanot was right: Europe was ready for a continent-wide club competition. It has now evolved into the phenomenally popular Champions League.

Hanot was also the brains behind the Ballon d'Or, the annual trophy awarded by France Football magazine to the best European player of the year. In 2010, this award was merged with FIFA's World Player of the Year and renamed the FIFA Ballon d'Or.

While France continues to produce players of the calibre of Paul Pogba, Antoine Griezmann and Anthony Martial, and as the country showed by hosting the highly successful 2016 European Championship in purpose-built or newly refurbished stadiums, it looks as if her influence on the beautiful game is set to continue for a long time to come.

Find the answers to these questions in the text

1 Who succeeded Henri Delaunay as head of UEFA?

2 What club competition was an inspiration for Gabriel Hanot when he thought up the European Cup?

3 Which of the Frenchmen mentioned in the article was nominated for a Nobel Peace Prize?

4 What is the name of the trophy awarded to winners of the European Championship?

5 Which French magazine used to award the Ballon d'Or?

6 Gabriel Hanot was editor of which French daily newspaper?

7 Whose suggestion was it to invite countries from all over the world to play in the World Cup?

8 Who invited representatives of the major European federations to a meeting in Paris in 1903?

The Passive

> **"** In the course of time, it **will be said** that Maradona was to football what Rimbaud was to poetry and Mozart to music. **"**
>
> —ERIC CANTONA

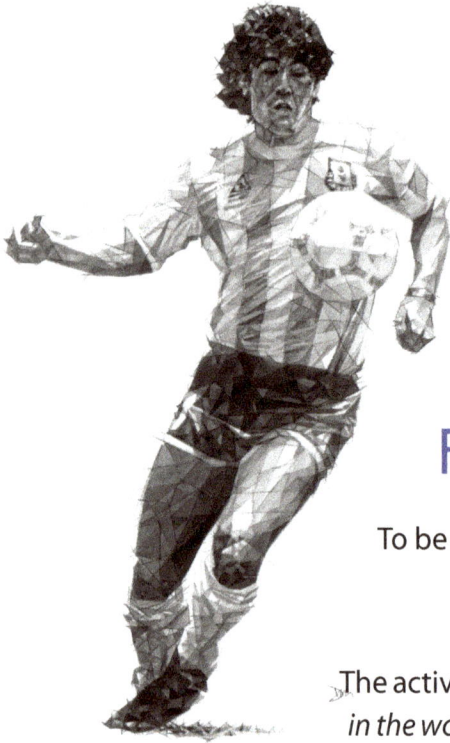

We use the passive when we want to talk about an action but we are not so interested in saying who or what does/did the action, or we don't need to because it's obvious from the context. If we use the passive and we want to say who the agent is, then we can use *by*.

Forming the Passive

To be + past participle:

*Football **is played** in every country in the world*

The active form of this sentence would be: *People play football in every country in the world*. But it's obvious that it's people who play football; we just want to communicate the fact *football – played – in every country,* so we use the passive.

Present simple passive (am/are/is + past participle):

*The Copa América **is held** every four years.*

Present continuous passive (am/are/is + being + past participle)

*Many new stadiums **are being built** for the 2022 World Cup in Qatar.*

Present perfect passive (has/have + been + past participle)

*The World Cup **has been won** by the host nation on six occasions.*

Past simple passive (was/were + past participle)

*George Best **was rejected** by his local club for being too small and skinny.*

Past continuous passive (was/were + being + past participle)

*He felt he **was being targeted** for abuse by the home supporters.*

Past perfect passive (had been + past participle)

*He couldn't play for England as he **had** already **been called up** to play for Scotland.*

Future (will be + past participle) passive

*The fixture list for next year **will be published** tomorrow.*

Future (going to be + past participle) passive

*The draw for the quarter-finals of the Champions League **is going to be held** in Sion next week.*

Modal (modal + be + past participle)

*A player **can be sent off** for protesting too much.*

Infinitive (to be + past participle)

*Football **used to be considered** a game that only working class people followed.*

Gerund (- ing + past participle)

*To avoid **being sent** to jail, the Leeds United player volunteered to do community service.*

We can use *get* instead of *to be* in passive structures. This use is generally more informal.

*He **got sent off** again.*

*The grass **gets watered** 5 times a week.*

*'If players don't want **to get kicked**, they should become accountants.' –Roberto Mancini*

⚽ **DID YOU KNOW?** ⚽

Law 13 states: 'If a direct free-kick **is kicked** directly into the team's own goal, a corner kick **is awarded** to the opposing team.' It doesn't count as an own goal.

Complete the following sentences with the phrases in the box

be worshipped	get injured	was banned	sent off	were beaten	having been
was composed	is claimed	was stopped	was ranked	were named	

1 After Napoli won the 1987 league title, in one central parish 25% of newly born boys ____ ____ Diego.

2 Celtic's European Cup-winning team of 1967 ____ ____ entirely of Glaswegians.

3 Norway ____ ____ second in FIFA's world rankings in October 1993.

4 'Whoever invented football should ____ ____ as a God.' – Hugo Sánchez

5 It ____ ____ that Edmundo got an ape drunk at his son's birthday party.

6 Jonathon Woodgate scored an own goal and was ____ ____ on his (quite disastrous) Real Madrid debut.

7 Romario, ____ ____ criticised by Pelé, described the Brazil legend as 'mentally retarded'.

8 Antoine Griezmann ____ ____ from the French international setup for 14 months after he and some team-mates left their hotel in Le Havre to go to a nightclub… in Paris.

9 The most common time in games for players to ____ ____ are the two 15-minute periods at the end of both halves.

10 In two separate incidents – in 2008 and 2013 – Marek Hamšík ____ ____ at gunpoint by masked criminals while driving his car in Naples and ordered to hand over his €10,000 Rolex.

> " *I told myself before the game , he's made of skin and bone just like everyone else — but I was wrong.* "

—TARCISIO BURGNICH, THE ITALIAN DEFENDER WHO MARKED PELÉ IN THE 1970 WORLD CUP FINAL.

When he was a child, Pelé and his friends were in a gang called the Shoeless Ones. They used to play with old socks filled with paper for a ball. They stole peanuts from a shop and sold them outside a cinema until they had enough cash to buy shoes, shirts and a ball.

He scored four goals on his league debut for Santos in a match against FC Corinthians, on 7 September 1956.

At the 1958 World Cup in Sweden, a 17-year-old Pelé ended up with the number 10 shirt when FIFA randomly handed out the numbers after the Brazilian Federation forgot to send in their squad list on time. He wore the same number for the rest of his career.

The Brazilian government declared Pelé an official national treasure in 1961 to prevent him from being transferred out of the country.

On 21 November 1964, he scored eight goals when Santos beat Botafogo 11-0.

In 1967, a 48-hour ceasefire was declared in Nigeria so the Federal and Rebel troops could watch Pelé play on a visit to the country.

He popularised the phrase 'o jogo bonito' after he published an autobiography with the title *My Life and the Beautiful Game* in 1977.

There have been many books, songs and poems written about him, and several films made. He stars as himself in the 1979 movie *Os Trombadinhas*.

He scored his 1000th goal against Vasco da Gama at the Maracanã in Rio. The following day's newspapers, which in every other country on the planet covered nothing but the second Apollo moon landing, were split down the middle in Brazil: Apollo 12 on one side, Pelé on the other.

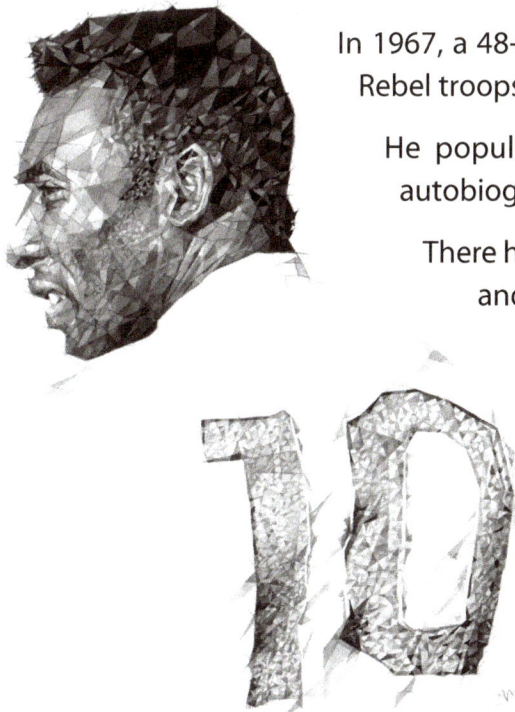

He was appointed Minister for Sport in Brazil in 1995, serving until 1998.

He was given an honorary British Knighthood in 1997.

Pelé has been a singer and a composer. He composed the entire soundtrack for the film *Pelé* in 1997. He has acted in several movies.

He was voted Athlete of the Century by the International Olympic Committee in 1999.

His father Dondinho, who played semi-professionally, once scored five headed goals in one game. As for Pelé, four headers was the most he managed to score in one match.

At Santos, 19th November is known as 'Pelé Day', to celebrate the anniversary of his 1,000th goal.

Brazil never lost a game when Pelé and Garrincha lined out together for the national side.

He worked as a scout for English club Fulham in 2002.

In 2008, he was robbed at gunpoint. Even though he told the gang who he was, they took his jewellery and phone.

In 2014, his son Edinho was sentenced to 33 years in prison for laundering money from drug trafficking. Pelé maintains he is innocent.

What they said about him:

'The greatest player in history was Di Stéfano. I refuse to classify Pelé as a player. He was above that.'

—FERENC PUSKÁS

'I remember Saldanha the coach being asked by a Brazilian journalist who was the best goalkeeper in his squad. He said Pelé. The man could play in any position.'

—BOBBY MOORE

'When I saw Pelé play, it made me feel I should hang up my boots.'

—JUST FONTAINE

'Pelé was one of the few who contradicted my theory: instead of 15 minutes of fame, he will have 15 centuries.'

—ANDY WARHOL

'My name is Ronald Regan, I'm the President of the United States of America. But you don't need to introduce yourself, because everyone knows who Pelé is.'

—RONALD REGAN

'Pelé was the only footballer who surpassed the boundaries of logic.'

—JOHANN CRUYFF

EXERCISE

State whether the following statements are *true* or *false* according to the text

1 Pelé played for English club Fulham.

2 '*O jogo bonito*' means 'the beautiful game' in Portuguese.

3 The Brazilian government wanted Pelé to play his football in Brazil and not abroad.

4 He wore the number 10 jersey throughout his career because 10 is his lucky number.

5 He scored his 1000th goal at the Maracanã stadium.

6 He was shot by robbers in 2008.

7 Brazil won every match in which Pelé and Garrincha played together.

8 His first professional game was against FC Corinthians.

9 He has written music.

10 He once scored 5 headers in a game.

Used to and Would

> " If I had an argument with a player, we **would talk** about it and then decide I was right. "
>
> —LEGENDARY MANAGER BRIAN CLOUGH

Used to

We use *used to + infinitive* to talk about past repeated actions or habits, and states or situations which no longer exist.

> Eric Cantona **used to play** for Manchester United (this sentence tells us that for an unspecified period of time Cantona played for Man Utd, and that he no longer does).
>
> Brazilian legend Gérson **used to smoke** sixty cigarettes a day.

We use *didn't use to* for negative sentences.

> You **didn't use to be allowed** to make substitutions during a match. NOT ~~You didn't **used to**~~

We do not use *used to* if we want to talk about how long a situation lasts, or how often something happened.

> Eric Cantona played for Manchester United for four and a half years.
> NOT ~~Eric Cantona used to play for Manchester United for four and a half years.~~

Used to doesn't exist in the present tense. For present habits, we use the present simple, and if we want to emphasise the habitual nature of our actions, we use *usually* or *normally*.

> We usually meet our friends in the same pub before matches. NOT ~~We use to meet…~~

In a formal style, *used to* can have the forms of a modal auxilliary verb, i.e. we form negatives and questions without *do*.

> **Did you use to watch** Match of the Day when you were a kid? (informal)
>
> **Used you watch** Match of the Day when you were a kid? (formal)
>
> She **didn't use to like** football, but now she loves it. (informal)
>
> She **used not/usen't to like** football, but now she loves it. (formal)

Would

We also use *would* to talk about past repeated actions and events, but more when we want to reminisce about the past or to show that we're being nostalgic. We also use it to talk about tendencies and characteristic behaviour in the past.

*My grandad and I **would** often **go** to the stadium an hour before the match started. We **would** often **be** the first people there.*

We don't normally use *would* with state verbs (*like, love, hate,* etc).

*I **used to love** when the fans started singing You'll Never Walk Alone. NOT ~~I would love when…~~*

Would isn't used in the negative or in yes/no questions.

*I **didn't use to buy** a matchday programme, but I'd sometimes pick up a discarded one on my way out. NOT ~~I wouldn't buy…~~ (this means I refused to buy a programme)*

*Did you **use to go** to away matches too? NOT ~~Would you go …?~~*

Neither *used to* or *would* can be used to describe a single action in the past.

Arsenal moved into the Emirates Stadium in 2006. NOT ~~Arsenal used to move into…~~

> ## ⚽ DID YOU KNOW? ⚽
>
> Fabio Cannavaro **used to be** a ball boy. He was one of the ball boys for the World Cup semi-final between Argentina and Italy in Naples at Italia '90.

EXERCISE 👟

Put the following words and phrases into the correct sentences

wear	would	be accompanied	to go	shower	change	fall	known	used	to be

1 Carlos Bilardo, Argentina's World Cup-winning manager at Mexico '86, used ____ ____ a gynaecologist.

2 Fans of Ajax star Sjaak Swart would ____ ends at half time in order to be able to follow their favourite player more closely.

3 Carlos Bilardo, when asked about his team selection for Mexico, ____ answer: 'Maradona and ten others.'

4 Football ____ to be a much slower game.

5 Atlético Madrid used to be ____ as Atlético Aviación de Madrid.

6 Until 1909, goalkeepers used to ____ the same strip as their outfield team-mates.

7 In Brazil in the early days of Futsal, the five-a-side form of football, there was a rule which stated that a player couldn't play the ball if his hand was on the floor. Players would ____ in bizarre ways to make sure their hands didn't touch the floor, which led to a huge increase in fractures.

8 Ary Barroso was the most famous radio commentator in Brazil in the '40s and '50s. His match reports would ____ ____ by him playing his harmonica. He was also one of Brazil's most successful songwriters in the first half of the 20th century.

9 Giovanni Trapattoni would sometimes ____ his players from the touchline with holy water.

10 'I used ____ ____ missing a lot … Miss Canada, Miss United Kingdom, Miss World.' - George Best, always fond of the ladies.

In 1976, Chris Nicholl of Aston Villa scored all four goals in a 2-2 draw with Leicester. Yes, two goals for his side, and two own goals for Leicester. He asked the referee for the match ball at the end of the game - players are usually allowed to keep the ball if they score three or more goals in a match – but the ref informed him that he was keeping the ball himself as it was his last game as an official.

As part of the BigShoe project, Mesut Özil donated his 2014 World Cup winnings, an estimated £240,000, to pay for 23 sick Brazilian children to have medical surgery as a 'personal thank you for the hospitality of the people of Brazil'.

Vitaly Daraselia, who scored the winner for Dinamo Tbilisi against Carl Zeiss Jena in the 1981 Cup Winners Cup final, was killed in a car crash in 1982. David Kipiani, who had provided the assist in the final, also died in a car crash in 2001.

There were 250,000 requests for tickets from across Europe to watch the 1928 Amsterdam Olympics football final between Uruguay and Argentina. Such demand led to the agreement to launch the World Cup.

Igor Belanov's wife was arrested for shoplifting when he was a Borussia Mönchengladbach player.

Rudi Gutendorf has had an incredible career as a manager. He has coached fifty-five teams, among them 20 national teams. When he was forty-six years old and manager of Chile, he had an affair with a teenage Miss Chile. He was shot at with a machine gun while he was driving his jeep through the countryside. Some time later he had another affair with a much younger woman. One night, when the two of them were lying in bed, a gunman broke in and opened fire on them. A bullet went through Gutendorf's jawbone and his lover was killed instantly. It is thought that she worked for the CIA.

When the 11-year-old Alexandre Pato broke his arm, it was discovered that he had a tumour. It was touch and go whether the arm would have to be amputated. Fortunately for him, the surgery was successful and he didn't need to have an amputation.

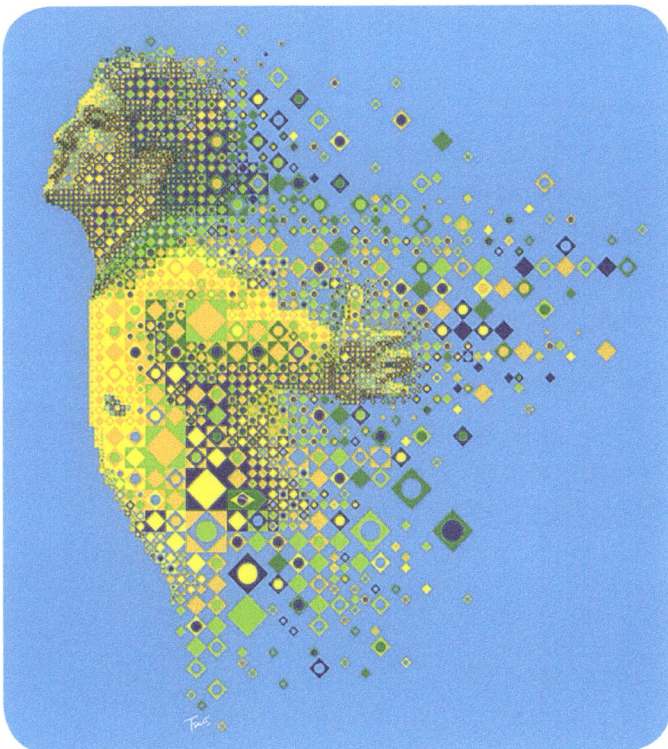

Maradona won the Golden Ball having been voted the best player at the 1986 World Cup. The trophy he was presented with was later stolen and melted down into gold bars on the orders of a mafia don.

When Christian Vieri signed for Inter in 1999, the price of milk in Milan rose by 15 per cent. This was because the chairman of Inter, Sergio Cragnotti, was also the owner of the main milk company, and ordered the price increase to cover the costs of the player's transfer fee and salary.

Alex Villaplane, Captain of France at the 1930 World Cup in Uruguay, was later shot by the French Resistance for collaborating with the Nazis.

Hristo Stoichkov marched into the triumphant opposition's changing-rooms after the Bulgarian cup final and smashed the trophy to pieces on the wall as the players celebrated in the bath.

It has been claimed that AC Milan president Silvio Berlusconi used to be a fan of city rivals Internazionale. Berlusconi has always denied this, saying that 'I have never been an Inter fan, you can't change your religion.' It has been proven, however, that in 1980 he had actually tried to buy Inter. As some mischievous journalists have pointed out, only a fan of Inter could possibly want to buy the club, knowing its tortured history of disappointments.

Every FIFA World Player of the Year since 1996 has played for either Barcelona or Real Madrid during their careers.

In 1936 Josep Sunyol, president of Barcelona, was driving outside Madrid when he was captured and shot by Franco's forces.

In 2003, a football supporter in Brazil, identified only as Roberto, tied himself to a tree outside the stadium of the club he supported, Corinthians. He refused to come down unless the team changed their tactics and formation, and fed himself with a bag of bananas he had brought up with him. He stayed up in the tree for a week, throwing the banana skins at the players as they walked below him. At first they in turn threw rotten fruit at him, but then they just ignored him. 'The players kept sticking their fingers up at me,' complained Roberto.

Esteemed mathematician Harald Bohr, brother of the Nobel Prize-winning physicist and chemist Nils Bohr, played for the Danish national football team, with whom he won an Olympic silver medal at the 1908 Olympic Games. Such was his popularity as a footballer, that when he defended his doctoral thesis the audience was reported as having more football fans than mathematicians. Nils Bohr himself played for the club Akademisk Boldklub – which was also Harald's club - as reserve goalkeeper.

Say whether the following sentences are *true* or *false*

1   Rudi Gutendorf was shot dead in Chile.

2   In 2003, a supporter of Corinthian's spent a week up in a tree.

3   Christian Vieri once affected the price of milk in Milan.

4   Every winner of FIFA's World Player of the Year award has played for either Real Madrid or Barcelona.

5   Vitaly Daraselia and David Kipiani both died in car crashes.

6   Chris Nicholl wasn't given the match ball because he only scored two goals for his own side.

7   Nils Bohr played international football for Denmark.

8   Maradona won the Golden Ball having finished top scorer at Mexico '86.

9   Around a quarter of a million people wanted to watch the 1928 Olympic football final.

10   It's quite likely that in the past Silvio Berlusconi was a fan of Inter.

Verb + to-infinitive, Verb (+ preposition) + -ing

> " *Iniesta is the boyfriend that every mother **wants** her daughter **to have**.* "
>
> —SERGIO RAMOS

When we use two verbs together, the form of the second verb depends on the first verb. The second verb can be the *to-infinitive*, the *infinitive without to* (also known as the *bare infinitive*), or the *-ing* (also known as the *gerund*).

Verb + to-infinitive

Here's a list of verbs which are followed by the *to-infinitive* and which don't need an object.

afford	agree	aim	appear	arrange	attempt	be able	be likely	claim
decide	deserve	expect	fail	hope	learn	manage	offer	plan
pretend	promise	refuse	seem	tend	threaten	try	want	

*Mario Götze **decided to return** to his former club,*
Borussia Dortmund, where he had enjoyed happier times.

Some verbs are always followed by an *object + to-infinitive*.

advise	allow	convince	encourage	force	get	persuade	remind	teach	tell	warn

*The referee **told him to stop** arguing with him.*

*The manager **persuaded the Board of Directors to**
give him one more season to try to improve the team.*

Some verbs can be used with or without an *object + to-infinitive*.

ask	choose	dare	expect	help	intend	need	prefer	prepare	want

*A club like Juventus **expects to win** every home game.*

*It's hard to be a professional sometimes – the supporters **expect us to perfom** miracles every week.*

Verb (+preposition) + -ing

Here are some verbs that are followed by *-ing*.

admit	avoid	approve of	can't help	can't stand	carry on	consider	deny
don't mind	enjoy	feel like	finish	give up	hate	imagine	include
insist on	involve	keep	like	dislike	love	mention	mime
mind	miss	practise	put off	recommend	resist	suggest	think of/about

*I **can't help daydreaming** about us winning the league.*
*I **keep visualising** our captain lifting the trophy at the end of the season.*

When a verb is followed by a preposition (except *to*), then the following verb is always *-ing*.

*I think the club has **given up trying** to co-operate with the Ultras.*

EXERCISE

Choose the correct option to complete the sentences

to fold/ folding	to analyse/ analysing	to be/being	to cut/ cutting	to rock/ rocking	to score/ scoring
to break/ breaking	to play/ playing	to go/going	to leave/ leaving	to warm up/ warming up	

1 Danish goalkeeper Michael Stensgaard retired in 1999 after suffering an injury to his shoulder while he attempted _____ down an ironing board.

2 Maradona refused _____ to the 2006 World Cup opening ceremony. 'I'm not here to look at bloody Pelé walking around,' he said.

3 60 Seconds is a street game where the goalie kicks the ball out, the others then have to cooperate _____ with a volley within 60 seconds.

4 Former Feyenoord manager Wiel Coerver invented a training system that involved _____ footage of great players in action and _____ down their moves into stages that could be taught.

5 When Bebeto scored against the Netherlands in their 1994 World Cup match, he mimed _____ a baby, as his wife had just given birth to a boy.

6 In 2003, Everton's Richard Wright twisted his ankle falling over a sign that warned players not _____ in the goalmouth.

7 When the other clubs found out that Bayern Munich had gone behind their backs to negotiate their own TV deal, Bayern threatened _____ the Bundesliga and play in Italy's Serie A if they were punished.

8 The Argentine striker Claudio Caniggia was not selected for national duty for several years after refusing _____ his long hair.

9 'The ball is like a woman, she loves _____ caressed.' - Eric Cantona

10 Former US Secretary of State Henry Kissinger convinced Pelé _____ football in the United States.

Tall tales in Montevideo

We're in the Fox and Hound, a popular pub with the _expatriate_ community in Montevideo, Uruguay. Sitting on a high stool at the bar and enjoying his usual _tipple_ of vodka and tonic is Luiz, local _barfly_ and _bon vivant_. He has just finished watching the big local derby - Peñarol v Nacional - on the television above the bar. Standing around him at the busy counter are three friends from Northampton in England: Mark, Jason and Pete.

'_Take whatever he says to you with a pinch of salt_,' says the barman to the three Englishmen, conspiratorially and _out of earshot_ of Luiz. 'He makes everything up. _He'd talk the hind legs off a donkey_, too.'

The three friends nod and _chuckle_ to themselves.

'Did you know,' starts Luiz, and now facing the three guys, 'did you know that during a match in Brazil, I don't know when or where exactly, but during some match in Brazil a supporter stopped a definite goal being scored by shooting the ball before it had crossed the line? I'm serious. The ball popped and just fell to the ground, the bullet had passed right through it.'

Mark: Come on man, _pull the other one_, that's mad!

Luiz: You don't believe me? It's true, I tell you, true. And another time an angry mob _lynched_ a referee in Brazil. They drove over him repeatedly on a motorbike till his head fell off.

Pete: _You're winding us up_ now, mate. Till his head fell off! Haha, _come off it_!

Luiz: Or did you hear about the time supporters of Boca Juniors…no, wait, it was Independiente…got into the stadium of their rivals Racing Club de Avellaneda when they were out celebrating winning some cup or other or playing in a tournament. They _buried_ seven cats under the pitch.

Jason: Ha, _you're having a laugh_.

Luiz: No, really. And Racing Club spent years looking for the seventh cat – they'd found the other six over that time, but couldn't locate the seventh. They _blamed_ it for their lack of success. They'd even got a priest to perform an exorcism of the stadium.

Mark: No way!

Luiz: Eventually they decided to _excavate_ an old _moat_ that went around the pitch, and that's where they found the seventh cat. They went on to win the league the following season, for the first time in years. They'd lifted the curse.

Pete: We believe you, thousands wouldn't.

Mark: Sounds like another _whopper_ to me.

Luiz: In Africa, there are cases where teams buried skulls in the centre circle, to put a curse on the other team.

Jason: Get outta here! Skulls!

Luiz: Yes, they're wonderfully superstitious in Africa. Before a tournament in the 1980s, the Ivory Coast squad was encouraged by their witch doctors to whisper their wishes into the ear of a living pigeon.

Mark: Pigeon! I'm not buying that one, no way.

Jason: I've heard footballers speaking _pidgin English_, but never heard them chatting to pigeons.

Luiz: Oh, and I heard this the other day. In Africa, one time, lightning struck a pitch during a match and one of the teams - the entire team - was killed. No-one on the other side was even injured. That's the god's honest truth!

Pete: Yeah, right, sounds _legit_. The entire team!

Luiz: No, really. It might have been something to do with the footwear the other team was wearing. Oh, and check this out: one time my friend Claudio was in Madagascar and he went along to a league game. It finished 149-0, I'm serious, 149-0. They were all own

goals scored in protest at a refereeing decision in a previous game. Claudio's not one for making up stories either, I should add.

Mark: I'm sure *he's* not. Own goals? Are you sure the other team hadn't been hit by lightning or something?

Jason: Have you any stories for us about European football?

Luiz: Of course. Let me think. Oh yes, there was the 'gull' kick, in Holland.

Pete: What was that, then?

Luiz: In a match in the Dutch League, the Feyenoord goalkeeper kicked the ball out so high it hit a passing seagull, knocking the bird out of the sky and killing it. They had it _stuffed_, it's in their club trophy room now.

Jason: Haha, 'gull' kick, you've gotta love it.

Luiz: Speaking of animals affecting games, there was that incident during a match in England in the 1970s. A sheepdog ran onto the pitch, collided with a goalkeeper and broke the keeper's knee. It ended his career. Pretty unlucky, right?

Pete: Likely story. Ended his career? Are you sure it wasn't a mammoth?

Mark: Or a unicorn.

Luiz: No, it was definitely a dog. Must have been running really fast. And have you ever heard about that Leeds United manager who had to touch a bus stop before every home match? Yes, indeed. It's not only Africans or South Americans who are superstitious. He also believed Leeds' stadium was cursed by gypsies.

Jason: Never heard it, no.

Luiz: Then there was that player in Italy who, when he was sent off, _snatched_ the red card out of the referee's hand and proceeded to eat it. That's no word of a lie.

Mark: Was it made from pasta or something? That's _preposterous_!

Luiz: Oh, and have I told you the one about…

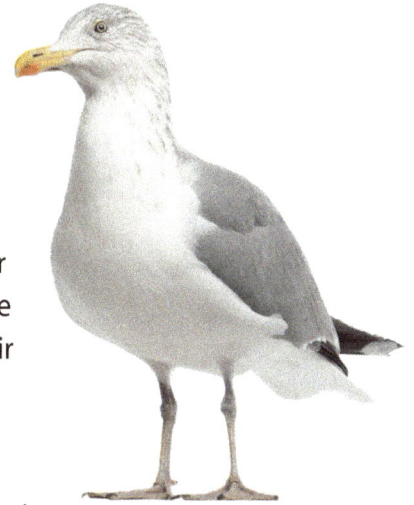

EXERCISE

Find the underlined words or phrases which mean the following

1　Filled with material.

2　Taken aggressively.

3　An informal term for an alcoholic drink.

4　Slang for 'a lie'.

5　To dig up the ground to try to find something.

6　Ridiculous, not credible.

7　A person who lives abroad.

8　Don't take seriously what someone says.

9　A very basic form of English, often combining English words with words from another language.

10　He talks a lot.

11　You're playing with us, teasing us.

12　Slang for 'credible'.

13　You're joking.

14　Someone who spends a lot of time drinking in bars.

15　Murdered by an angry group of people.

16　Someone who enjoys the nice things in life, especially food and drink.

17　A defensive hole dug around a place we want to protect.

18　Charged with being at fault.

19　We don't believe you.

20　Stop joking with us.

21　Not within hearing distance.

22　Laughed in a quiet manner.

Note: All of Luiz's stories are in fact true!

DISCUSSION 🔔

Do you know any other bizarre stories about football?

Verbs which can be followed by a gerund or an infinitive

> " Goals are like ketchup. Once they **start flowing** they come in sudden bursts, all at once. "
>
> —RUUD VAN NISTELROOY

Some verbs can be followed by a gerund (-ing) or an infinitive (with *to*) **with a change of meaning**:

Remember + infinitive = you remember first, then you do something.

> *If we get a penalty, **remember to kick** the ball to their goalie's left. It's his weaker side.*

Remember + gerund = you do something and then you remember it. (often used when we reminisce)

> *I **remember crying** my eyes out when Brazil lost against Italy in Spain '82.*

Forget + infinitive = you don't remember to do something. (often used to talk about neglecting to carry out a duty)

> *If you **forget to apply** the tactics we covered in training, you'll be dropped for our next game.*

Forget + gerund = don't have any recollection of doing something. (the opposite when it's negative)

> *I'll never **forget playing** with my friends out on our street. Those were the days.*

Try + infinitive = make an effort to do something.

> *No, he **tried to pull** out of the tackle. He did not deliberately injure the player.*

Try + gerund = experiment to see if something works.

> *I've **tried leaving** five minutes before the end of a match, but I still get caught up in the traffic.*

Some verbs can be followed by the infinitive or the gerund *without* **a change of meaning**, e.g. *continue, begin, start*.

Like, *love*, *hate* and *prefer* can also be followed by either a gerund or an infinitive. We use the gerund when we're talking generally, and the infinitive to talk about more specific situations.

*I only **like to go** to away games when a group of my friends are going.*

*I **like watching** Champions League matches over at my cousin's house.*
His fridge is always well stocked with beer.

Need is normally followed by an infinitive.

*You **need to be** patient. You can't expect a new manager to turn things around straight away.*

Sometimes, however, it can be followed by a gerund. This is a passive structure.

*That pitch **needs mowing**. The grass is way too long! (= that pitch needs to be mowed)*

EXERCISE

Complete the following sentences using a word from the box

| needs | forget | beat | stop | remember | watching | seeing | leaving | know | doing |

1   Don't _____ to record the Champions League highlights programme for me later.

2   I've tried _____ the room when my team has a penalty kick, but it hasn't really changed how successful the players are at converting them.

3   Milner keeps trying to _____ Dani Alves, but he just can't get around him, he's not quick enough.

4   _____ to test out their new keeper as soon as you can, he looked dodgy when he made his debut last week. Shoot on sight!

5   He's tried _____ yoga, he's tried swimming every day, but so far nothing is helping him lose his back pain.

6   'I only need to _____ a hundred words of English to manage the England team.' –Fabio Capello

7 I distinctly remember _____ my uncle cry when Liverpool came back to beat AC Milan in the 2005 Champions League final.

8 I'll never forget _____ the awful events of Hillsborough unfold before my eyes.

9 That ref _____ sacking. He's made seven or eight terrible decisions today.

10 'Once they said they could only stop me with a pistol, but today you need a machine gun to _____ Messi.' –Hristo Stoichkov

Adverbs of Frequency

> " He's a lucky guy, Cristiano, he **always** gets first row tickets to see Messi win his awards. "
>
> —ZLATAN IBRAHIMOVIC

Adverbs of frequency tell us how often something happens or is done. They can be allocated into three groups: adverbs of definite frequency (e.g. *yearly*), adverbs of indefinite frequency (e.g. *sometimes*) and adverbial phrases (e.g. *every so often*).

Adverbs of Definite Frequency

Adverbs of definite frequency – hourly, weekly, twice a year, once etc – typically go in the end position (the end of a clause).

*Most clubs pay their players **monthly**.*

*The management team meets **weekly** to discuss the team's performance.*

Sometimes, usually for reasons of emphasis or style, some adverbs of definite frequency go at the front.

***Every fortnight**, 75,000 paying spectators come to Old Trafford to watch Man Utd play.*

Adverbs of Indefinite Frequency

Adverbs of indefinite frequency usually come before the main verb, but after the verb *to be* and after the first auxiliary verb.

*Corporate guests **hardly ever** arrive on time for a game.*

*Jack Wilshere is **always** out injured.*

*Like the great Italian defender Scirea, he has **never** been sent off in his career.*
NOT He has been never sent off…

ADVERBS OF FREQUENCY • 77

These are the most common adverbs of indefinite frequency:

**always, constantly, often, frequently, usually, normally, generally, regularly,
sometimes, occasionally, rarely, infrequently, not often, seldom, hardly ever, never.**

Sometimes, often, occasionally, frequently, rarely, usually and *normally* can go at the beginning or end of a clause too.

> *'When I think I've made an error, it can cause me a sleepless night.
> But that only happens **rarely**.' –Louis Van Gaal*

Always and *never* can come at the beginning of imperative clauses.

> ***Never** buy a ticket from a tout.
> You'll be ripped off.*

Always, usually and *normally* are not used on their own to tell you how often something happens.

> *Do you go to every home game?* ~~Yes, usually.~~
>
> *Yes, as much as possible.*

DID YOU KNOW?

Arrigo Sacchi, coach of the exceptional A.C. Milan side of the late 1980s and early 1990s, **never** played professional football himself. 'You don't have to be a horse to be a jockey,' he famously said.

Adverbial Phrases of Frequency

The usual position of an adverb phrase – e.g. *now and again, once in a blue moon, five times a day, on Saturday afternoons, every year* - is at the beginning or end of a clause, not in the middle.

> ***Every so often**, the scouts at Flamengo find a real gem of a player, or what Brazilians call a 'craque'.*

Note: 'On Sunday' refers to one day, 'on Sundays' means 'every Sunday'.

EXERCISE 👟

Complete the sentences with a word or phrase from the box

never	once a week	always	continually	hardly ever	usually
never	always	sometimes	again	years	

1 'If you were a racehorse, you'd have been put down years ago. You're _____ fit.' – Brian Clough to Leeds Utd player Peter Lorimer

2 He _____ leaves the ground a few minutes before full-time in order to avoid the crowds. It depends on how the match is going.

3 They _____ play a 4-4-2 system. Now and _____, the manager changes it to a 4-5-1.

4 Arsenal are the only English team to have _____ been relegated.

5 I'm not surprised he was booked, he was _____ fouling his marker.

6 I'd prefer it if the World Cup was held every two _____. Four years is such a long time to have to wait.

7 '_____ look on the bright side of life.' –The popular Monty Python song which is often sung by fans when their team is losing.

8 'I don't like journalists and I _____ _____ talk to them.' – Mario Balotelli

9 'For me that cup will _____ be covered in blood. The cup of death.' – Juventus player Antonio Cabrini, speaking about the 1985 European Cup final at the Heysel Stadium, Brussels.

10 'My worst vice is gluttony. I try to keep myself under control because I'm an athlete, but _____ _____ _____ I like to pig out and act like a normal person.' – Gigi Buffon

Clichés

Cliché: a phrase or opinion that is over used and betrays a lack of original thought.

Arsenal are playing Everton in a Premier League tie. Clive Isley (A) and Ray Broughton (B) are commentating.

A: *What a glaring miss! He's blazed it over the bar when it would have been easier to score.*

B: *He's got to be hitting the target from there.*

A: *It sat up perfectly for him,* too.

B: *He's almost hit it too well,* Clive. *He can't buy a goal at the moment,* can he?

A: Well, it looks like that's the last of the action Giroud sees today. They're taking him off and bringing on Özil. How do you rate the German's season so far, Ray?

B: Well, *you're never sure what you're going to get with him,* are you? *On his day, he's virtually unplayable.* But for me *he goes missing in the big games.*

A: *He's got to step up to the plate now. We need to see some end product from him.*

B: Indeed, *Arsenal need to start turning these draws into wins.*

A: Another corner to Arsenal. *The big lads are coming up from the back. Everton are up against it now. Arsenal are really piling on the pressure.*

B: Third corner in a row, *it's backs to the wall time.*

A: Oh, that's a shocking challenge by Baines on Özil, an awful two-footed lunge. Completely *over the top.*

B: I'm surprised at Baines, Clive, *he's really not that kind of player.* What's the ref going to do now? Just a yellow, *he's a lucky boy.*

A: *There's no place for that in football.* He could have seriously injured the player. Free kick now for Arsenal. Özil is back on his feet, thankfully. Sánchez is standing over the ball, too. Özil shoots. GOAL! What a screamer! One-nil to the Arsenal!

B: What a strike! It's no more than they deserve, Clive. It's been coming for a while now. Fantastic strike!

A: Can Everton come back from this? We're into stoppage time now.

B: They really need to go for an equaliser. *They don't want to get dragged into a relegation dogfight. No-one's too big to go down.*

A: *The table doesn't lie, they're just above the drop zone* because they've been so inconsistent all season.

B: You wouldn't know it by their manager's expression. *He's calmness personified* as usual.

A: *No doubt the two managers will be discussing* Özil's goal *over a bottle of red after the game,* Ray, whatever the result.

EXERCISE

The phrases in *italics* in the text are examples of the type of cliché commonly used by football commentators. Can you find the clichés which mean the following?

1 It's a challenging period when everyone involved must try their hardest.

2 He's not contributing much to his team in important matches.

3 This striker is going through a barren spell.

4 He needs to take responsibility.

5 Just because a club is famous or has been successful doesn't mean they can't be relegated.

6 He doesn't show much emotion.

7 Close to the bottom places in the league table.

8 A player who is so good that it's impossible to stop him from inflicting damage on you when he's playing to the best of his ability.

9 The ball bounced up to the perfect height for the player to connect with it.

10 He's not normally a dirty player.

DISCUSSION

Do you have similar clichés in your language?

Be/Get Used To

> " I've been booed in Holland and in Uruguay — as a professional footballer you need to have thick skin and just **get used to** it. "
>
> —LUIS SUAREZ

To be used to + noun or gerund (...-ing)

If you say that you are *used to something/doing something*, you mean that you have experienced it enough that it is no longer strange to you. You are accustomed to it.

> *I'm used to the Liverpool accent – I've been playing for Everton for six seasons now, so I understand the locals perfectly well!*

> *Are you used to living in Spain now? Their culture is quite different from yours.*

In the past

> *He wore gloves because, coming from Ecuador, he wasn't used to the freezing German winters.*

In the future

> *This time next year, Gareth Bale will be used to life in Spain.*

Be careful not to confuse this structure with *used to do something* (see the unit *Used to and Would*). The meaning is completely different.

To get used to + noun or gerund

Get used to means *become used/accustomed to*. We can use *get used to* to talk about the process of becoming used to or accustomed to something. When the process is still ongoing we use the continuous form *getting*. We use *get* or *got* to talk about the finished process.

In the present

I'm getting used to German food. There are still a few things I haven't tried, and I really miss my mother's tortilla espanola. (This means he is not fully accustomed to German food. He's still going through the process of becoming accustomed to it, it's still a bit strange to him.)

*It can be challenging, but most players **get used to** their fitness regimes (they reach the point where it stops being too difficult).*

*'**Have** you **got used** to not being able to stand on terraces in English stadiums?' 'No, not really. I think there should be at least one section of the ground where supporters can watch the match standing, as there is in Germany. The atmosphere in grounds isn't as good as it was in the past.'*

In the past

*It took my Arsenal-supporting friend Ken some time **to get used to** his team playing at the Emirates. For a long time, he still called the ground by its old name, Highbury. But he **got used to** it eventually.*

*It's such a pity he got injured, I really felt he **was getting used to** playing in that new midfield role.*

In the future

*'I really don't like the new home kit. That sash looks ridiculous.' 'You always moan when we change strips. I'm sure you**'ll get used to** it. It's really not that bad.'*

EXERCISE

Complete the sentences with a word from the box

| getting | he's | will | I'm | were | got | would | to | haven't | couldn't | was |

1   They crashed out of the Champions League as too many of their players _____ not used to such a big stage.

2   'Do you think Juventus supporters _____ get used to seeing their club in Serie B?' 'Well, I doubt they'll be there too long. Two seasons at the most.'

3   I still _____ got used to the fact that Alex Ferguson is no longer Man Utd's manager, he was there so long, wasn't he?

4   He left English football after only one season as he _____ get used to the physicality. Also, he _____ used to the slower pace and higher levels of technique in Italy.

5   'Do you think viewers _____ get used to it if the television stations started showing short adverts during games?' 'No, not here, people wouldn't put up with it at all.'

6   I never thought I'd say this, but I think I am actually _____ used to the weather here. It's stiflingly hot in the afternoon, but I just take a siesta and when I wake up it has cooled down.

7   I was surprised by how quickly goalkeepers _____ used to the new backpass rule. It was a big change for them. Suddenly they had to be able to play a bit like a sweeper.

8   He found all the adulation a bit odd at first, but I think _____ used to it now. He might even miss it when he retires.

9   That's the third time he's been in a car crash since he arrived in England; it's about time he got used _____ driving on the opposite side of the road, isn't it?

10   When they converted our ground into an all-seater stadium it did initially seem a bit strange, but _____ used to it now.

The Mystery of the Jules Rimet Trophy

At the organisation's 1929 Barcelona congress, FIFA President Jules Rimet awarded Uruguay the right to host the following year's inaugural World Cup tournament, and he commissioned a trophy – then known as the Goddess of Victory and only later, in 1946, as the Jules Rimet Trophy (or Coupe Jules Rimet) – from French sculptor Abel Lafleur. It was to be made of gold plated sterling silver and lapis lazuli, and depicted Nike, the Greek goddess of victory.

Jules Rimet, both man and trophy, were aboard the Conte Verde when it set sail for Uruguay, departing from the south of France on 21 June 1930. The French, Belgian and Romanian football teams were also on board.

During World War 2, Italian Football Federation secretary Ottorino Barassi secretly transported the trophy from a bank in Rome, and kept it out of Nazi hands by hiding it in a shoebox under his bed and then in chicken coops. It has been claimed that the Nazis searched his apartment looking for the trophy, but overlooked the shoebox. (Italy were the cup-holders having won the 1938 World Cup, the last before war broke out.)

It was renamed the Jules Rimet Trophy in 1946 in honour of the former FIFA president.

Jules Rimet himself presented the trophy to the Uruguay captain when they famously won the 1950 World Cup at the Maracanã in Rio de Janeiro.

When England staged the World Cup in 1966, they put the trophy on display at Westminster Central Hall, from where it was stolen. Fortunately, the cup was found a week later by a black and white collie dog named Pickles, who found it wrapped in newspaper beneath a bush in south London. The Football Association, paranoid that it might disappear again, secretly had a replica of the trophy made. It was this replica that victorious England captain Bobby Moore was presented with.

Pickles became a celebrity and even made a brief appearance in the British comedy The Spy With a Cold Nose. Sadly, he strangled himself on his lead while chasing a cat in 1967.

Brazil won the World Cup for the third time in 1970, and so were awarded permanent custody of the trophy. FIFA commissioned a new cup, which was first presented to West Germany in 1974, and it is known simply as the FIFA World Cup Trophy. It's the same cup that Germany were presented with on winning the 2014 World Cup in Brazil.

In 1983, the original cup was stolen from the Brazilian Football Federation offices in Rio. It has never been recovered and the official police line is that it was melted down into gold bars and sold, but there is no actual proof to verify this. In fact, the story seems implausible as the trophy wasn't made of gold, it was just gold-plated.

In 1996, David Baddiel and Frank Skinner, two famous English comedians, wrote the lyrics to England's official anthem for that year's European Championship. The song, Three Lions, memorably featured the phrase 'Jules Rimet still gleaming', a reference to England's 1966 World Cup victory.

The replica trophy that the English association had made in 1966 was put up for auction in 1997. An anonymous bidder paid a staggering £254,500 for it. It turned out that this bidder was in fact FIFA. They paid so much for it because they believed that it was the original Jules Rimet trophy: they thought the trophy that was given to the Brazilians to keep for good in 1970 was the replica, and that the FA had kept the original all along. It turned out that FIFA was wrong about this: the cup they purchased at auction was in fact the replica. (See highly regarded football writer Simon Kuper's articles: 'My quest for football's Holy Grail' and 'What happened to the lost World Cup?').

Others have claimed that the trophy disappeared as far back as 1957 or 1958 while in German hands, and that there are photographs which show that the cup presented to Brazil in 1958 is different from the 1954 trophy. Martin Atherton has written a book, *The Theft of the Jules Rimet Trophy*, and there's a documentary by Lorenzo Garzella, Filippo Macelloni and César Meneghetti called *Rimet Trophy*, in which they try to get to the bottom of the mystery surrounding the cup.

The truth is no-one knows for sure where the original Jules Rimet trophy is, and it's likely that its whereabouts will remain a mystery forever.

EXERCISE

Say whether the following sentences are *true* or *false* according to the text

1   If a country wins the World Cup three times, FIFA allows them to keep the trophy on a permanent basis.

2   FIFA believed that the English FA kept the original Jules Rimet trophy they had won in 1966 and gave them a replica ahead of Mexico '70.

3   Pickles was a cat.

4   The original Jules Rimet trophy was made of solid gold.

5 In 1983, The Brazilian FA threw out the cup by mistake.

6 The European teams travelled to the 1930 World Cup by ship.

7 Pickles took the trophy from Westminster Central Hall.

8 The first World Cup tournament was held in 1930.

9 David Baddiel and Frank Skinner played for England at Euro '96.

10 The cup presented to the winners of the World Cup is still known as the Jules Rimet trophy.

DISCUSSION

What do you think really happened to the Jules Rimet trophy?

Can and Be Able To for Ability and Possibility

> **❝** Apart from Kahn, you **could** put that lot in a bag and beat it with a stick and whoever got hit would deserve it. **❞**

—FRANZ BECKENBAUER, UNIMPRESSED WITH THE 2002 GERMAN WORLD CUP TEAM.

	can	**be able to (+infinitive)**
present simple	can	am/is/are able to
future (will)	-	will be able to
past simple	could	was/were able to
present perfect	-	has/have been able to
conditional	could	would be able to
infinitive	-	(to) be able to
gerund	-	being able to

Ability

Present

We use *can* to talk about present or general ability. *To be able to* is also possible for general ability.

> *We **can** still win this, there are six minutes of additional time.*

> *José Mourinho **can/is able to** speak at least five languages fluently.*

Can is a modal auxiliary verb. There is no *s* in the third person singular, and questions and negatives are formed without *do*.

Future

We use *will/won't be able to* to talk about future ability. We don't use *can*.

> *In the future, players **will be able to** recover from injuries much more quickly.*
> *NOT ~~will can recover~~*

However, we use *can/can't* if we are deciding now about the future.

> *'I **can't** come to the match tonight'. 'That's a shame. **Can** you come to the next one?'*

Past

We use *could* to talk about general ability in the past (*was/were able to* is also possible), to say that we could do something at any time, whenever we wanted.

> *We **could** easily afford to go to games when we were kids, it was so cheap.*

However, we do not use *could* to say that we did something **on one occasion**. We use *managed to* + *infinitive, succeeded in* + *gerund,* or *was/were able to* + *infinitive.*

> *He **managed to** squeeze the ball past Courtois from an almost impossible angle.*
> *NOT ~~He could squeeze the ball…~~*

But we can use *couldn't* to say that we did *not* succeed in doing something on one occasion.

> *I **managed to** find the right section of the stand, but I **couldn't** find my seat number.*

Managed and *succeeded* are usually only possible in the positive.

Conditional

We use *could* to mean *would be able to* in conditional sentences.

> *We **could** win the league if only we kept our best players. We really are a selling club, aren't we?*

As a general rule, use *be able to* + *infinitive* when there is no form of *can*, e.g. in the present perfect or infinitive.

> *Despite his goal-scoring record, **he's never been able to** win over the supporters.*

> *I'd like **to be able to** go on an away trip to a European match some time.*

We use *could have* + *past participle* to say we had the ability to do something but we didn't try or want to do it, or circumstances prevented us from doing it.

> *When Zidane signed for Madrid, he **could have joined** any club he wanted to.*

Possibility

We use *can* to say that situations and events are possible.

*Football games **can** be a bit boring. (can used in this way means sometimes)*

*They **can't** get drawn with Roma again his year, **can** they?*
They've been in the same group three out of the last four seasons.

*Apparently, there's going to be a special guest performing at half-time tomorrow. Who **can** it be?*

We use *could* to talk about general possibility in the past.

*It **could** be intimidating to stand on the old Kop at Anfield, it was so crowded and noisy.*

Could have + past participle is used in the same way as might/may have + past participle.

*Ferguson has dropped Beckham. **Could they have fallen out** again?*

EXERCISE

Put the words or phrases into the correct sentence

be able	can't be	have been	could do	can	saved
can't	could win	could have	can do	could	be

1 'It's not Alf's fault – nobody _____ _____ the World Cup with those players'. – TV pundit Jimmy Hill on England manager Alf Ramsey's chances of winning the 1966 World Cup, which, of course, England went on to win.

2 'You _____ _____ out of the game for two years and then come back in a tournament like the World Cup'. – Denis Law, criticising Italy manager Enzo Bearzot for picking Paolo Rossi for his 1982 World Cup-winning side. Rossi ended up being the tournament's top scorer.

3 When Italy got the result they needed against Cameroon at the 1982 World Cup, there were suggestions that there could _____ _____ something fishy going on. Some Italian journalists claimed that the wife of the Cameroon manager boarded a plane with a bag full of foreign money.

4 'When the Dutch say that someone _____ play football, they are referring exclusively to his technique and his reading of the game. Courage, desire to win, pace and height mean nothing to them.' – Simon Kuper, writer.

5 'It happened and I _____ pretend it wasn't me.' – Zinedine Zidane, following his headbutt on Italian player Materazzi in the 2006 World Cup final.

6 'I want to _____ _____ to open a cupboard without a football player falling out,' César Luis Menotti, Argentina manager, confirming that he was still planning to retire after winning the World Cup in '78.

7 'I thought Buffon _____ _____ saved that one.' 'No, I always think that if a shot can be _____ Buffon will save it.'

8 'On sand you can never _____ sure of anything' – Eric Cantona, who really got into beach football after he retired from the 11-a-side game.

9 'We _____ win the World Cup without scoring a goal in open play.' – Republic of Ireland manager Jack Charlton, who was overheard saying this during Italia '90. Ireland reached the quarter finals without scoring in open play.

10 'What Zidane _____ _____ with a football, Maradona _____ _____ with an orange.' – Michel Platini

Random Football Tales 3

In a Danish league match between Ebeltoft and Nørager, referee Henning Erikstrup was about to blow for full-time when his dentures fell out. While he was scrambling around on the pitch looking for his false teeth, Ebeltoft scored an equaliser. Ignoring the protests from the Ebeltoft players, and with his dentures now back in place, Mr Erikstrup disallowed the goal and then blew the final whistle.

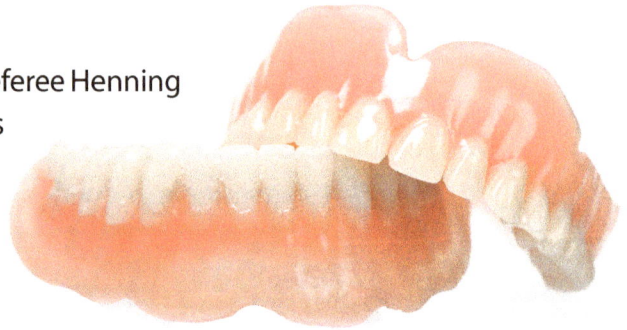

Lower-league English side Congleton Town FC had announced in their match-day programme that a minute's silence would be observed before kick-off to mourn the death of the club's oldest supporter, Fred Cope, who had passed away that week. Just as the players were lining up around the centre circle with their heads bowed, the club officials learned that not only had Mr Cope not died, but he had just arrived in the stadium for the game. Realising their embarrassing mistake, and having to think of something quickly, they announced that the tribute was in fact for England World Cup-winning captain Bobby Moore, who had died a few days before.

West Ham defender Alvin Martin scored a hat-trick against three different goalkeepers in his side's 8-1 victory over Newcastle in 1986. The injured Martin Thomas was replaced in the Newcastle goal first by Chris Hedworth, then by Peter Beardsley.

When Luis Monti lined out for Italy in the 1934 World Cup final, it was in fact his second consecutive World Cup final appearance. He had played for Argentina against Uruguay in 1930. It was common practice back then for Italy to call up players who were born or brought up in other countries but who were descendents of Italian emigrants, even when these players were already playing for or had already represented different national sides. They called these players *oriundi*.

In the 1930 World Cup semi–final between the USA and Argentina, US coach Jack Coll ran onto the pitch to remonstrate with the referee. In the process, he knocked over his medical bag, breaking a bottle of chloroform. He collapsed to the ground as he'd accidentally anaesthetised himself.

Kaká's career almost ended at the age of 18 when he jumped off a diving board into a swimming pool and fractured his spine.

On 24 July 2004, Young Tigers coach Michael Sizani was shot dead by the referee during a match against Mighty Eleven Chiefs in Kenton-on-Sea, a town in the Eastern Cape district of South Africa. Sizani was leading his players over to the ref to complain about a penalty decision when the referee, 26-year-old Ncedisile Zakhe, took out the gun which he had concealed in his pants, and fired one shot. The bullet which killed Sizani also injured the opposition coach and an opposition player. Zakhe then jumped over the stadium fence and fled the scene. He was subsequently caught and sentenced to six years in prison for culpable homicide.

In the 1938 World Cup semi-final, legendary Italian striker Giuseppe Meazza's shorts fell down as he was about to take a penalty kick. The elastic had been ripped by an opposing defender. Holding up the shorts with one hand, he managed to retain his composure to slot the ball away. His celebrating team-mates surrounded him to provide the necessary cover until a new pair of shorts was produced.

EXERCISE

Say whether the following sentences are _true_ or _false_ according to the text

1 Peter Beardsley has never played in goal.

2 Foreign players of Italian extraction who played for Italy were known as _oriundi_.

3 Referee Ncedisile Zakhe was shot dead during a match in South Africa in 2004.

4 Bobby Moore was captain of England when they won the World Cup in 1966.

5 One of Henning Erikstrup's contact lenses fell out during the Ebeltoft v Nørager match.

6 Alvin Martin scored all eight of his side's goals in their victory over Newcastle in 1986.

7 Luis Monti played in two World Cup finals for two different countries.

8 Jack Coll knocked himself out during a 1930 World Cup match.

Word Search

Find in the grid ten people you would see on a football pitch or in a team's technical area. The first one is done for you

E	S	T	R	I	K	E	R	S
P	U	K	A	J	C	X	I	W
S	B	W	I	N	G	E	R	E
F	S	Z	T	T	I	Q	P	E
U	I	A	O	I	E	P	A	P
L	D	C	U	Y	W	H	R	E
L	O	E	S	B	U	Y	L	R
B	C	H	E	K	F	S	J	B
A	T	N	M	O	N	I	D	R
C	O	A	C	H	I	O	U	A
K	R	K	E	E	P	E	R	S
C	X	V	B	V	X	F	P	X
Z	M	A	N	A	G	E	R	Z

Phrasal Verbs

> In 1969, I **gave up** alcohol and women. It was the worst 20 minutes of my life.

—GEORGE BEST

The term *phrasal verb* usually refers to all multi-word verbs, consisting of a verb and one or more particles. There are four basic types of phrasal verb.

1   Intransitive (doesn't take a direct object)
Verb + particle

*The match **kicked off**.*

2   Tranitive (takes a direct object) and separable

    a   Verb + direct object + particle or

    b   Verb + particle + direct object

       *The referee **sent off** the player. OR*
       *The referee **sent** the player **off**.*

    a   is favoured if the noun phrase is particularly long, e.g. The manager **pointed out** all the unnecessary defensive mistakes and poor decision making to his players.

When the direct object is a pronoun, however, it *must* go between the verb and particle.

*The referee **sent** him **off**. NOT ~~The referee **sent off** him.~~*

3   Transitive (takes a direct object) and inseparable
We always put the direct object – noun or pronoun – after the particle.
Verb + particle + direct object

*No club wants to **go through** a relegation. NOT ~~**go** a relegation **through**.~~*

A good dictionary will tell you which verbs are transitive or intransitive. Some phrasal verbs can be both, *e.g. to go through.*

    a   *Rangers have **gone through** several difficult seasons since they were relegated from the Scottish Premier League.*

    b   *The managers are looking tense; they know only one team can **go through**.*

Many dictionaries show you when a phrasal verb is separable. If a dictionary writes *look (something) up*, you know the phrasal verb *look up* is separable, i.e. you can say *look something up* or *look up something*. If the verb is written *look for (something)*, we know it's not separable.

4   Phrasal verbs which have more than one particle
We always put the direct object – noun or pronoun – after the final particle.

Verb + particle + particle + direct object

*Some players don't **get on with** their team-mates. NOT **get on** their team-mates **with**.*

Many phrasal verbs have more than one meaning, for example we can ***pick up** an injury/the ball/habits/a language/points.* Again, a good dictionary should help you here.

A lot of phrasal verbs have a more formal-sounding, Latin-derived, one-word synonym. It's usually more appropriate to use the phrasal verb in informal writing and conversation.

To light up = to illuminate
To rule out = to disallow
To put out = to extinguish (e.g. a fire)
To send off = to dismiss
To break up = to disassemble

*Messi **lights up** every game he plays in.*
*NOT Messi **illuminates** every game he plays in.*

Phrasal verbs can often have an idiomatic meaning, i.e. the meaning of the multi-word verb is different from the meaning of the parts taken separately.

*In the past, supporters **put up with** much worse facilities. (Put up with is not the same as put + up + with).*

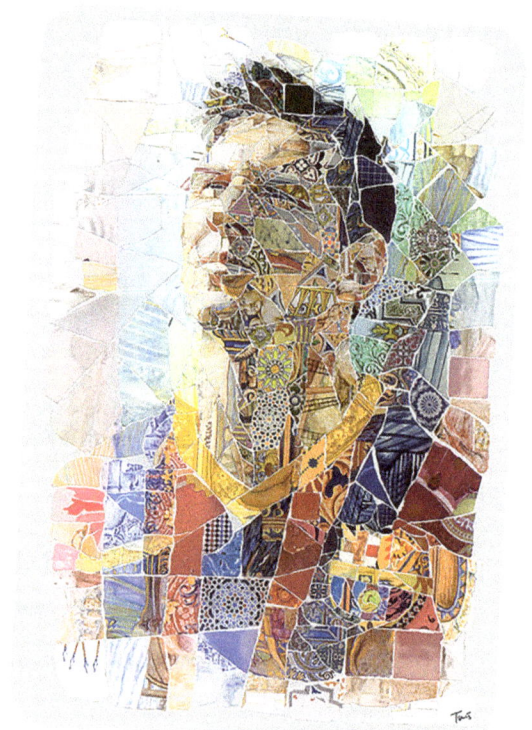

> ⚽ **DID YOU KNOW?** ⚽
>
> The Brazil national team were **put through** the same conditioning programme as NASA's astronauts to prepare them for the high altitudes at Mexico '70.

Glossary

to kick off = to start

to send off = to expel from the pitch

to go through (trans) = to experience

to go through (intrans) = to qualify

to get on with = to have a good relationship with someone

to put up with = to tolerate

EXERCISE

Put the phrasal verbs in the box into the correct form to complete the sentences

put on   walk off   set up   turn down   go through   play on   get over   send off   go off   turn up

1   On his international debut for Argentina, Lionel Messi was ____ ____ after 47 seconds.

2   When he played for Man Utd, superstitious Paul Ince always had to be the last player to ____ ____ his jersey before running out onto the pitch.

3   Manchester City goalkeeper Bert Trautmann broke his neck during the 1956 FA Cup final and yet ____ ____ until the end of the match.

4   In October 1995, Shakhtar Donetsk's president Alexander Bragin and four of his bodyguards died when a bomb ____ ____ in their stadium during a home game against Tavriya Simferopol.

5   Sócrates ____ ____ £1 million contracts with Roma and Juventus because of clauses that forbade him to make love for 3 days before a match.

6   It's estimated that up to 90,000 people ____ ____ to see Maradona being presented at Napoli's San Paolo stadium after he was signed in June 1984.
   a   Scottish schoolteacher, Alexander Hutton, ____ ____the Argentine Association Football League (AAFL) in 1893.

7   Shortly after Czechoslovakia went 2-0 down against Belgium in the football final of the 1920 Antwerp Olympic Games, they decided that the English ref was biased and so ____ ____ the pitch.

8   Ajax goalkeeper Stanley Menzo had to receive counselling to help him ____ ____ the trauma of being dropped by Louis Van Gaal in 1993.

9   'I don't ____ ____ life cursing the fact that I didn't win a World Cup. I played in a fantastic team that gave millions of people watching a great time.' – Johann Cruyff

Roberto Antonio Rojas and La Fogueteira

Some players will go to any lengths, legal or otherwise, to ensure their team gets the right result. Think Maradona and his infamous 'Hand of God' goal against England at the 1986 World Cup. Or Thierry Henry spinning away to celebrate William Gallas's goal for France in their World Cup play-off game against Ireland, his face betraying not the least sign of guilt for having handled the ball, not once but twice, in the move leading up to the goal.

Managers, too, are willing to bend the rules to gain their side an advantage, and they seem to spend much of their time trying to defend the indefensible, or like Arsène Wenger, claiming not to have seen the latest indiscretion by one of their charges.

But not even Henry or Maradona have taken matters into their own hands quite so literally as Chilean goalkeeper Roberto Antonio Rojas. He was known to his fans as the Condor, though Conman might be more apt.

On 3 September 1989, he was in goal for his country when they faced Brazil in a decisive World Cup qualifier at the Maracanã in Rio. Brazil only needed a draw to qualify and were leading comfortably 1-0 well into the second half. Twenty minutes from time, Rosenery Mello do Nascimento Barcelos da Silva – an attractive 24-year-old Brazilian woman – threw a firecracker onto the pitch. It landed close to Rojas, who went to ground, covering his face with his hands. With his face covered with blood, he was carried off the pitch by his team-mates and into the dressing room. The Chile team refused to finish the match.

FIFA launched an inquiry and, having viewed footage of the incident, found that Rojas hadn't been hit by the firecracker at all, but had deliberately cut his own face with a razor blade he had smuggled onto the pitch in one of his gloves. He was hoping the match would be abandoned so his team would get a replay. He received a lifetime ban (lifted by FIFA in 2001). Chile coach Orlando Aravena and team doctor Daniel Rodriguez were also banned for life. A Chilean inquiry found that Aravena ordered Rojas by walkie-talkie to remain on the ground. Brazil were awarded the game. Chile were knocked out and also banned from the following World Cup.

Rojas went on to coach at São Paulo. At the time of writing he is goalkeeping coach for Sport Club do Recife.

And if you think all this is bizarre, what happened to Rosenery da Silva is another one for the 'you couldn't make it up' file. She ended up becoming a kind of celebrity, earning herself the nickname *La Fogueteira* (the pyrotechnician) and a modelling contract with Brazilian Playboy worth a reputed $20,000.

Say whether the following statements are *true* or *false*

1 Rojas was nicknamed La Fogueteira.

2 In a play-off game against Ireland, Thierry Henry scored a goal with his hand.

3 Rojas didn't stay out of football forever.

4 If Chile had equalised before the end of the match at the Maracanã, they would have qualified for the 1990 World Cup.

5 People in the stadium recognised Rosenery da Silva as she was a famous model in Brazil.

6 Chile weren't allowed to play in the 1994 World Cup.

7 Other members of Chile's staff knew that Rojas was only pretending to have been struck by the firecracker.

8 FIFA decided to record the game as a draw.

Devilishly Difficult Quiz

How much do you know about World football? Test your knowledge here with our end of book quiz!

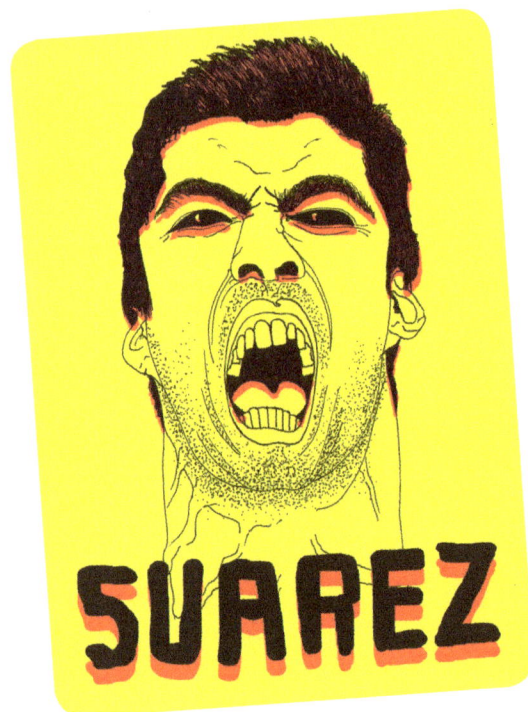

1 Which Japanese club did Arsène Wenger manage?

2 How many European Cup/Champions League finals did Paulo Maldini play in?

3 The most famous derby in Egyptian football is the fixture between Al Ahly and which other club?

4 Which club plays at La Bombonera?

5 Which club is Garrincha most associated with?

6 Who is the all-time record goalscorer in international football?

7 Real Madrid beat Eintracht Frankfurt 7-3 in the 1960 European Cup final. Two players scored all of Madrid's goals. Who were they?

8 The Porto Alegre derby is played between Internacional and which other club?

9 Who was known as the Galloping Major?

10 Who is the all-time record goalscorer in a single UEFA Cup/Europa League season?

11 Which African nation lost most of its squad in an air disaster in 1993?

12 Which South American club has won the most Copa Libertadores titles?

13 Who was voted FIFA Coach of the Century in 1999?

14 How many World Cup finals did Czechoslovakia play in?

    a 0

    b 1

    c 2

15 Who is Italy's all-time leading goalscorer?

16 Who was voted FC Barcelona's best player of all time in 1999?

17 Diego Maradona played for Napoli for how many seasons?

   a 3

   b 5

   c 7

18 Which national side were once known as the Wunderteam?

19 Which two countries are referred to as *rioplatense*?

20 Alfredo Di Stéfano played four seasons for a Colombian club. Who are they?

21 What does the word Borussia mean?

22 Everyone knows Real and Atlético, but can you name another club from Madrid?

23 Which English Premier League club are known as the Eagles?

24 What is so exceptional about the derby fixture between Galatasaray and Fenerbahçe?

25 Why does Sergio Agüero have 'Kun' written on the back of his shirt?

26 Which was the first World Cup finals in which substitutes were allowed?

27 Which trophy is nicknamed La Orejona in Spanish?

28 Who is the all-time top goalscorer in the UEFA Cup/Europa League?

29 Who is the only man to have won the World Cup twice as a manager?

30 In what city was Stade de Colombes located?

31 Only one club has been an ever present in Italy's Serie A since its founding. Who are they?

32 Which European club plays at the Marakana?

33 Which two clubs compete in the Derby della Madonnina?

34 The top goalscorer at the end of the season in La Liga is awarded the Pichichi trophy. Which club did Pichichi play for?

35 Pelé and Franz Beckenbauer played for which American side?

36 Which Italian club's badge features an image of a she-wolf suckling a pair of infants?

37 With which other Serie A club do Genoa share their ground?

38 In which city are Servette located?

39 Who is the only outfield player to have appeared in five World Cup finals?

40 In which national league do Ebusua Dwarfs and Hearts of Oak play?

41 The football club Fotballaget Fart is based in what country?

42 Which derby is known as the Derby d'Italia?

43 Which Spanish side is nicknamed the Mattress Makers?

44 In what country would you find the football club called The Strongest?

45 Who is credited with introducing football to Brazil?

46 Ajax > Barcelona > Los Angeles Aztecs > Washington Diplomats > Levante > Ajax > Feyenoord is which player's club career path?

47 Which top-flight Belgian club uses an emblem of an Native American chieftain to represent the club?

48 Kalamazoo Outrage existed between 2007 and 2010. In what country was this club based?

49 How many different clubs have won the Champions League/European Cup?

    a 22

    b 27

    c 32

50 Who was the last club to successfully defend its Champions League/European Cup title?

Practise asking questions in English by testing a partner with the questions above!

Exercise Keys

Present Simple and Continuous

1 know, (ii) missing
2 lives
3 use
4 know
5 means
6 Is
7 leaving
8 is
9 lifts
10 watch

Lionel Messi Factfile

1 True
2 True
3 False. He won the Golden Ball, not the Golden Boot.
4 False. Newell's Old Boys.
5 True
6 True
7 True
8 False. He cried all night.

Present Perfect Simple and Continuous

1 played
2 spent
3 won
4 described
5 melting
6 admitted, (ii) put
7 triumphed
8 paying
9 been
10 had

Staged Diving with Allan Simonsen

1 To flop
2 To fake
3 Bemusement
4 To turn a blind eye
5 Harm
6 To alert
7 Booked
8 To be inducted
9 What's the big deal?
10 A launch

Past Simple and Continuous

1 meeting
2 chose
3 thrilled
4 carried out, (ii) found
5 were, (ii) insisted, (iii) remained
6 could
7 reffing, (ii) acting
8 looking, (ii) standing up
9 scored
10 claimed, (ii) performing

Mixed-up Sentences: The Rules of Football

1 Players must wear a jersey, shorts, stockings, shinguards and footwear.
2 The ball crosses the goal line inside the goal mouth.

3 **a** The game can be played on either natural or artificial surfaces.

    b The surface must be green and rectangular in shape.

4 The referee ensures the Laws of the Game are respected and upheld.

5 Used to restart play after the whole of the ball has crossed the touch line.

6 All players must be in their own half prior to kick-off.

7 A game cannot start if either team has less than seven players.

8 **a** The game is played in two halves consisting of 45 minutes each.

    b The half time interval must not exceed 15 minutes.

9 Two yellow cards are equivalent to one red card.

10 A free kick can either be direct or indirect.

China and Football

1 Dismal

2 Puzzling

3 Compulsory

4 Depict

5 Land

6 Rife

7 Set up

8 Mull over

9 To be on the up

10 Fixed

Past Perfect

1 had, won

2 had expelled

3 had forgotten

4 had, taunting

5 (i) had played, (ii) had, able to

6 had suffered, (ii) had left, (iii) had, claimed

7 had, failed

8 had persuaded

9 had, introducing, (ii) had, selected

10 had said

A League of their Own

1 to ban

2 to get behind

3 a think tank

4 mooted

5 nowadays

6 lacking

7 a sponsor

8 to approve of

9 cutting your nose off to spite your face.

10 wiped out

11 to be up in arms

12 to start from scratch

13 shelved

14 scope

15 an exaggeration

16 a procession

17 in tandem with

18 took off

19 to envisage

20 a cradle

21 to come round to the idea

22 traitors

23 That has a certain ring to it

24 brand new

25 a coup

26 the yoke

'Will' for the Future

1 win
2 top
3 sing, (ii) boo
4 play
5 be, (ii) overcome
6 pay
7 come on
8 be able, (ii) be
9 speak
10 be

Random Football Tales

1 False
2 True
3 True
4 False. He became a stamp dealer
5 True
6 True
7 False. Size 10
8 False. Fenerbahçe
9 True
10 False. He was playing a joke

Future Continuous and Future Perfect

1 Broken
2 Travelling
3 Become
4 Won
5 Playing, banned
6 Earning
7 Won
8 Waiting
9 Won
10 Playing

Celebrations Gone Wrong

1 False. Curitiba.
2 True
3 False. He returned to football after his injury, eventually rejoining Boca Juniors.
4 False. He died in hospital.
5 True
6 True
7 False. The Champions League final.

Real Conditionals

1 isn't
2 is
3 know
4 shoot
5 score
6 have
7 is
8 hope
9 discussing
10 going

Jumbled-up Words: What's my Injury?

1 Torn hamstring
2 Broken metatarsal
3 Dead leg
4 Dislocated shoulder
5 Torn achilles tendon
6 Pulled thigh muscle
7 Fractured cheek bone
8 Concussion
9 Groin strain
10 Ruptured ligaments

Football on Film

1 Arty
2 Fond
3 To come to terms with
4 To portray
5 Sub-plots
6 Malapropism
7 Trawler
8 To get into
9 Foil
10 Vivid
11 In-jokes
12 Ponderous
13 To suspend your disbelief
14 Touching
15 To take on
16 Renowned
17 Shady
18 Grim
19 Edgier
20 Nit-picky
21 Sibling rivalry
22 Striving
23 Shot

Unreal Conditionals

1 take
2 could, score
3 tried
4 become
5 might, played, have, been
6 couldn't
7 complained
8 gave, done
9 had
10 would

France and Football

1 His son, Pierre.
2 The Mitropa Cup
3 Jules Rimet
4 The Henri Delaunay trophy
5 France Football
6 L'Équipe
7 Henri Delaunay
8 Robert Guérin

The Passive

1 were named
2 was composed
3 was ranked
4 be worshipped
5 is claimed
6 sent off
7 having been
8 was banned
9 get injured
10 was stopped

Pelé Fact File

1 False. He worked as a scout for Fulham.
2 True
3 True
4 False. He was randomly handed the number ten jersey by a FIFA official at the '58 World Cup
5 True
6 False. He was just robbed.
7 False. They didn't lose any games together, but they didn't win them all. Some games were drawn.
8 True
9 True
10 False. Four headed goals was his best performance. His father scored five headers in one game.

Used to and Would

1   to be
2   change
3   would
4   used
5   known
6   wear
7   fall
8   be accompanied
9   shower
10 to go

Random Football Tales 2

1   False. He was shot, but only injured.
2   True
3   True
4   False. Every winner since 1996.
5   True
6   False. He wasn't given the ball because the referee wanted to keep it for himself.
7   False. His brother did, but not him.
8   False. Golden Ball is awarded to the best player, not the top scorer.
9   True
10 True

Verb + to-infinitive, verb (+ preposition) + -ing

1   to fold
2   to go
3   to score
4   analysing, (ii) breaking
5   rocking
6   to warm up
7   to leave
8   to cut
9   to be
10 to play

Tall Tales in Montevideo

1   stuffed
2   snatched
3   a tipple
4   a porker
5   to excavate
6   preposterous
7   expatriate
8   Take whatever he says to you with a pinch of salt
9   pidgin English
10 He'd talk the hind legs off a donkey
11 You're winding us up
12 legit
13 you're having a laugh
14 a barfly
15 lynched
16 a bon vivant
17 a moat
18 blamed
19 pull the other one
20 come off it
21 out of earshot
22 chuckled

Verbs which can be followed by a gerund or an infinitive

1   forget
2   leaving
3   beat
4   Remember
5   doing
6   know

7 seeing

8 watching

9 needs

10 stop

Adverbs of Frequency

1 never

2 sometimes

3 usually, again

4 never

5 continually

6 years

7 Always

8 hardly ever

9 always

10 once a week

Clichés

1 It's backs to the wall time.

2 He goes missing in the big games.

3 He can't buy a goal at the moment.

4 He's got to step up to the plate now.

5 No-one's too big to go down.

6 He's calmness personified.

7 Just above the dropzone.

8 On his day he's virtually unplayable.

9 It sat up perfectly for him.

10 He's really not that kind of player.

Be/Get Used To

1 were

2 will

3 haven't

4 couldn't, was

5 would

6 getting

7 got

8 he's

9 to

10 I'm

The Mystery of the Jules Rimet Trophy

1 True

2 True

3 False. Pickles was a dog.

4 False. It was gold-plated, not made of solid gold.

5 False. It was stolen.

6 True

7 False. It was stolen.

8 True

9 False. They are comedians, not footballers.

10 False. It's now known as the FIFA World Cup Trophy.

Can and Be Able To for Ability and Possibility

1 could win

2 can't be

3 have been

4 can

5 can't

6 be able

7 could have

8 be

9 could

10 can do, (ii) could do

Random Football Tales 3

1. False. He went in goal to cover for his injured team-mate in the 8-1 defeat to West Ham in 1986.
2. True
3. False. He shot dead Young Tigers coach Michael Sizani.
4. True
5. False. His dentures (false teeth) fell out.
6. False. He scored a hat-trick, not all 8 goals.
7. True
8. True

Word Search

Answer, going across and down:

Striker, subs, winger, fullback, physio, doctor, coach, keeper, manager, sweeper

E	S	T	R	I	K	E	R	S
P	U	K	A	J	C	X	I	W
S	B	W	I	N	G	E	R	E
F	S	Z	T	T	I	Q	P	E
U	I	A	O	I	E	P	A	P
L	D	C	U	Y	W	H	R	E
L	O	E	S	B	U	Y	L	R
B	C	H	E	K	F	S	J	B
A	T	N	M	O	N	I	D	R
C	O	A	C	H	I	O	U	A
K	R	K	E	E	P	E	R	S
C	X	V	B	V	X	F	P	X
Z	M	A	N	A	G	E	R	Z

Phrasal Verbs

1. sent off
2. put on
3. played on
4. went off
5. turned down
6. turned up
7. set up
8. walked off
9. get over
10. go through

Roberto Antonio Rojas and La Fogueteira

1. False. He was known as the Condor.
2. False. He handled the ball in the build-up. Gallas scored the goal.
3. True
4. False. They needed to win.
5. False. She was unknown.
6. True
7. True
8. False. Brazil were awarded the victory.

Devilishly Difficult Quiz

1. Nagoya Grampus Eight, now known as Nagoya Grampus.
2. Eight
3. Zamalek
4. Boca Juniors
5. Botafogo
6. Ali Daei
7. Alfredo Di Stéfano and Ferenc Puskás.
8. Grêmio
9. Ferenc Puskás
10. Radamel Falcao
11. Zambia

12 Independiente

13 Rinus Michels

14 2

15 Luigi Riva

16 Ladislao Kubala

17 7

18 Austria

19 Argentina and Uruguay.

20 Millonarios

21 It's the Latin word for Prussia.

22 Rayo Vallecano, Getafe and CD Leganés

23 Crystal Palace

24 They are based in the same city but also on different continents: Europe and Asia.

25 It's the name of his favourite cartoon character from his childhood.

26 1970

27 The Champions League trophy. La Orejona means 'Big Ears' in Spanish, a reference to the very big handles on the trophy.

28 Henrik Larsson

29 Vittorio Pozzo

30 Paris (1938 World Cup final was held here, and it's also where some scenes in Escape to Victory were filmed)

31 Inter

32 Red Star Belgrade

33 AC Milan and Inter

34 Athletic Bilbao

35 New York Cosmos

36 AS Roma

37 Sampdoria

38 Geneva

39 Lothar Matthäus

40 Ghana Premier League

41 Norway

42 Inter v Juventus

43 Atlético Madrid

44 Bolivia

45 Charles Miller

46 Johann Cruyff

47 KAA Gent

48 USA

49 22

50 AC Milan in 1989/1990

Lightning Source UK Ltd.
Milton Keynes UK
UKHW051042060223
416527UK00009B/317